NEW
YORK
street food

TOM VANDENBERGHE,
JACQUELINE GOOSSENS & LUK THYS

NEW YORK

street food

Cooking & traveling in the 5 boroughs

LANNOO

Content

INTRODUCTION

To visit all the kinds of street food that exist in the world, you don't need to fly around the earth. You just can go to New York.

No other city on this planet houses so many nationalities in such great numbers. As a result, literally every world kitchen can be found in its streets. The supply of street food in New York nicely reflects the different food cultures. The influx of immigrants brings new dishes and influences that translate into what the streets have to offer.

Just as in Asia, Africa and Latin America, people sell their dishes on the streets with a lot of commitment, pride and passion. From the well equipped, almost gastronomical food trucks to a guy on a bike who sells tacos on a sidewalk of Flushing Avenue, or a funky gipsy-like cart in the Bronx...the variety of tastes, shapes and dishes is unrivaled.

The street food scene is quite dynamic, and not at all limited to the island of Manhattan. The locations of food stalls, carts and trucks shift in 'a New York minute' and also depend on the season. Trends follow each other in less than no time. Social media play a role in notifying **one** where your favorite food truck will sell its dishes that day. So a mobile internet phone is a handy tool to find those culinary treasures on wheels.

If you want to experience New York's street food scene, you have to travel a bit. Fortunately, the city has an efficient transportation system. With a little effort, you get to meet half of the world. The search for people and dishes that are authentic leads you to less obvious but fascinating parts of New York.

The American cuisine does not have the culinary traditions and anchoring of countries like France or China. But precisely because of this, there are fewer obstacles here. With no second thoughts the most diverse ingredients are brought together. This results in surprising dishes and boundary-breaking combinations. Tacos with kim chi (Korean fermented cabbage) or Belgian waffles with chili con carne. Eating is one of the greatest joys and virtues in New York, an adventure without borders!

NEW YORK CITY

New York City, with 8.3 million inhabitants, is the largest city in the US. It has five boroughs: Manhattan, Brooklyn, Queens, the Bronx and Staten Island. The most famous streets and neighborhoods, such as Wall Street, Times Square, Broadway, Harlem and Soho, are all on the island of Manhattan.

New York lies on a bay which forms one of the biggest natural harbors of the world. In 1624 the Dutch West-Indian Company founded a trading post on the southern end of Manhattan and called it Nieuw-Amsterdam. In 1665 the English took over and changed the name to New York. The city has always had an international flavor. In 2012, 40 percent of its population was born outside the US. This makes New York the most international city of the country and arguably of the world. Here you can eat every day in a different country without leaving the city. You can chose between 26.000 restaurants and thousands of food stands. They all are inspected by the New York City Department of Health & Mental Hygiene which has the reputation of being very strict.

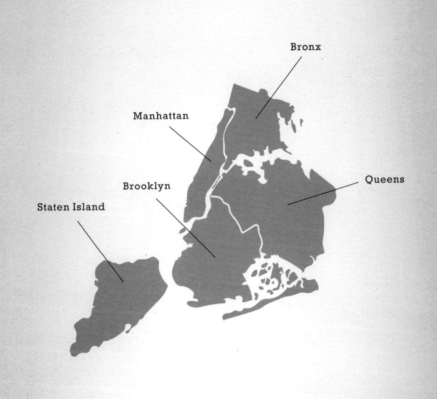

Bronx

Manhattan

Brooklyn

Queens

Staten Island

ABOUT TOM

Tom Vandenberghe is a passionate food adventurer. He is the soul of cooking studio 'Eetavontuur' ('Eating Adventure'). Recently, he started the noodle bar 'Ramen' in his home city Ghent (Belgium).

After writing a trilogy about street food in South East Asia (Bangkok, Hanoi, Singapore and Penang), Tom is still hungry. He lived for two years in Bangkok and Hanoi. For him, street food will always be closely associated with Asia. So he was very curious and in search of new culinary influences when he went to New York. There he discovered, with the aid of Jacqueline Goossens, new cuisines such as soul food and the Caribbean cuisine and tasted the influences of the South- and Central American culinary traditions. The deeper you dig, the more you want to know and taste. Tom takes pleasure in forging culinary links and the many meetings with kindred souls. He finds his kicks and joy of living in discovering new taste sensations, eating habits and culinary traditions.

He shares his passion for street food with his friend, food photographer Luk Thys. Through Luk, he met Jacqueline Goossens. Her encyclopedic knowledge of, and love for, New York were contagious; her social commitment heart-warming.

ABOUT JACQUELINE

Jacqueline moved to New York in October 1980. Since then, she has been working from there for various Belgian media. She wrote five books about her experiences in New York. This collaboration with Tom and Luk is her sixth. She lives with her partner, writer and visual artist Tom Ronse on the North Shore of Staten Island, which, in local political circles, is sometimes called 'the forgotten borough', and in rapper circles, Shaolin.

Jacqueline grew up in the town of Maldegem, in the Belgian province of East Flanders. She never forgot the taste of the homegrown food that was served at the table of her parents and grandparents. In New York, she still prepares the simple rural dishes that she learned from her grandma, combined with new ingredients that she keeps discovering in her thoroughly international city. Jacqueline likes to hunt, especially on her bike, for quality products at local markets, in ethnic neighborhoods and from street vendors. The collaboration with Tom and Luk was for her an unexpected opportunity to share her interest in culinary New York. She also thanks Tom Ronse, Annelies Van den Bleeken, Justin Ferate, Brit Uwaerts, Edwig Tanghe, Geert Ally and Michaël Mariën whose advice she sought for her contributions to this book.

ABOUT LUK

Luk is an experienced and renowned food and travel photographer with an international clientele. Many of his images are produced in his daylight studio in Ghent, where he collaborates with his business partner and colleague-photographer Bram Debaenst and a team of talented food stylists.

Tom Vandenberghe is his soul-brother. Together they roam the world, in search of the ultimate street food story and image. New York has further strengthened their bond. And, also thanks to Jacqueline's help, the vibrant city has proved to be a huge source of inspiration for them, which has further sharpened their street food hunger.

ABOUT THIS BOOK

When I presented my plans to write a book about New York, I often got the reaction that New York street food was just hot dogs, kebabs, pretzels and roasted nuts. Reason enough to investigate and roam the streets and neighborhoods in search of authentic dishes.
I already knew about the culinary diversity and the variety of the restaurant scene. During my local explorations, I was happy to see this culinary variety reflected in the streets as well. Street food is alive in New York. All sorts of people eat in the streets. From business suits lining up for food trucks in Manhattan, to factory workers buying from South American stalls and foodies in search of soul food in Queens or the Bronx. New York has a street-food scene as rich, diverse and inspiring as the city itself.
With good reason, food vendors are not always willing to reveal their recipes. It's their livelihood, their passport to the future. Often their income is based on recipes kept in the family for generations. Cooking is experimenting, interpreting recipes.

So in this book, we present our own interpretations of recipes we discovered and tasted in the streets.

This book does not aim to give a complete overview of street food in New York; it is but a snapshot. The city's is constantly changing; it is so extensive and diverse one could devote an entire life to its study. Still, we hope this book will give the general reader and amateur cook some insights into the New York street food scene. And we also hope to convince the reader to go beyond the beaten paths.
Our stay with Jacqueline and her knowledge of New York gave us the chance to get to know the city on a more personal level. I had countless meetings with native New Yorkers as well as with immigrants from all over the world, legally in the country or not. My experience of years spent traveling on different continents, as well as my culinary passion, allowed me to talk with each of them about their own local cuisine. I heard anecdotes and many family histories. Doors and kitchens opened for me. The contacts I had with these people were often fleeting yet never superficial. Food brings people closer together.
The streets of New York also touched me on a social level: people there help each other, whether you're looking to find the subway, a church or a food store. People join together, because they need each other or are in need of human contact. Perhaps all these colors and different nationalities in the streets make New York the model city for the future. A city where there is no difference between the native population and the immigrants. Where everybody tries to live together and everybody helps each other to survive in the urban jungle. Precisely because of this reason, we have not classified the recipes in this book according to ingredients, origin or cooking technique.

We clicked

One morning, when I was in Manhattan where I had several meetings to go to, I discovered I had forgotten my wallet. I had no cash or credit card, so I could forget about lunch. In the afternoon, I became increasingly hungry. Manhattan seemed to consist entirely of people eating in the streets, food carts, food trucks, restaurants and stores full of enticing take out dishes. I saw and smelled food everywhere. In a few hours, you'll be home I consoled myself, think of all those people who will go to bed hungry tonight. That helped just a little. Near the entrance of a subway station I saw a lady who looked like she was from Mexico or South America. She stood next to a shopping cart lined with a black garbage bag that more or less hid the cauldron in her cart. It's the classic equipment of the unlicensed street vendor who discretely sells homemade snacks. I showed the woman the two dimes which I found in my coat pocket. 'Can I buy something for this please? I'm so hungry and I forgot my money.' The woman gave me a sweet smile and two portions of churros, wrapped in paper. 'One is more than enough', I said but with a firm gesture she pushed the sweet fried dough sticks in my hands. All I could do was thank her. The combination of her generosity and the heavenly taste of those crispy churros is still my most beautiful street food memory.

I always felt a lot of sympathy for street vendors, in my home city as well as abroad. So I was immediately interested when professional foodie Tom Vandenberghe and his food photographer Luk Thys asked me to collaborate on a book on street food in New York. At first, I was a bit nervous. For years, I was used to roaming through the city on my own, in search of inspiration for my columns, stories and books. Now I would do that for several weeks in the company of two men I barely knew. On our first day I proposed to explore the street food scene in the South Bronx. I noticed immediately that both Tom and Luk were very relaxed during our subway trip. That was at least a good omen. Our first stop was a modest Dominican food stall. Tom greeted the saleswoman with the roguish smile that would melt many a street food vendor, men and women, during our subsequent trips. He ordered a snack, tasted attentively and asked the cook questions on how she prepared it. He ordered a drink of milk and orange juice. He gave the impression that he had all the time in the world. He fished his book *Hanoi Street Food* from his backpack and showed it to the woman, explaining that we wanted to make a similar book about street food in New York. Taking pictures was no problem. Luk asked if he could borrow the only chair and set out some dishes on it. He arranged and re-arranged his improvised mini-photo set. Some passers-by looked on with curiosity. Luk was not distracted. Tom occasionally made a suggestion. The two seemed perfectly matched. Our next stop was Maria's Tacos, a well known Mexican street kiosk, where Lucia Martinez is busy every day from 7 am. Tom again ordered several dishes and showed his book to Lucia. The cook nodded approvingly. The ice was broken. The two chefs chatted happily. Meanwhile, Luk was busy carefully arranging some copious *quesadillas*. I grabbed a table in the sun from where I could observe Tom and Luk. I felt we would work together smoothly. They were open-minded and showed respect for the vendors. And also, very importantly, they possessed a talent for improvisation and a sense of humor.

For our project, we crisscrossed New York's five boroughs. The culinary offerings in the streets reflected the soul of the city: very diverse, constantly changing with the most surprising fusions as a result.

TOM'S STORY

Just after the summer of 2012, while in need of a breather in my busy entrepreneur's life, I found a first occasion to immerse myself in New York's street food scene. Furthermore, I needed inspiration for a noodle bar concept in my home city Ghent. So for the fifth time in my wandering life, I bought a ticket to JFK International Airport. I couldn't think of a better destination. New York is an inexhaustible source of ideas, the ultimate trendsetter; a super concentrated chunk of human energy, visible from the moon.

While looking forward to new taste sensations and curious about the local street food scene, I moved into my room in Williamsburg, Brooklyn, booked through the site Airbnb. My culinary trip began with buying a week pass for the subway in the Flushing Avenue station. For about 30 dollars, I could go anywhere in the city all week long. My first trip was on the M train to Manhattan. The figures and letters of the trains dominate the lives of New Yorkers. They represent the hundreds of railway lines which run like pulsing veins through the city. If you live close to a subway station, you have better chances of survival in the urban jungle. It's as simple as that.

I get out near Bryant Park and walk to 34th Street. My goal is Korea town. K-town, as New Yorkers call it, is on the top on my list because the Korean cuisine is making an impact worldwide and rightly so. I'm excited when I enter my first Korean deli (a store where you can buy prepared dishes). This shop offers an ample buffet of very nicely presented platters, fresh looking vegetables, tofu, fish dishes, Korean prepared meat (**bulgogi**) and dishes made with **kimchi**, Korea's national dish of fermented cabbage. With my carefully chosen little dishes I go to the cash register. You pay per weight. In this case that means that I bought myself a balanced meal for just 7 dollars. The bulgogi is sublimely seasoned and still juicy; the veggies are crispy. Fresh, affordable and really tasty, I say to myself while, sitting on a stool, I enjoy my first meal of the day.

Back on the M-train, direction Brooklyn, a young guy plays on his saxophone. When I give him a dollar he thanks me with a friendly nod. I make a stop at 2nd Avenue. For years, I have dreamed of visiting David Chang's legendary noodle bar Momofuku. The restaurant exudes a laid back atmosphere. The food is top quality; every dish is beautifully balanced, seemingly simple yet subtle and complex. I choose Momofuku's interpretation of the Japanese noodle dish ramen. When I pierce the poached egg, the broth becomes deliciously creamy. A piece of pork belly melts in my mouth. I add a tad of siracha chili-sauce. While I eat, the view of the kitchen activities keeps me entertained. My eye catches a flyer on the counter. 'Round Table: From Markets to Carts, Street Food of New York'. I put the flyer in my pocket and go outside, satisfied. Back in my room in Williamsburg, I buy a ticket online for an event on the following day.

Like a real New Yorker, I begin the day with a cup of take-out coffee that is way too hot. Together with thousands of commuters I take the M-train to Manhattan as if I've been doing this for years. My first destination is on Park Avenue, a meeting place of street food trucks and an essential part of the midtown lunch scene. Right before 11 am, I see the Cinnamon Snail truck on 47th Street. I've been following Adam and his team for a while on Facebook. Now it's time for a real visit. Cinnamon Snail serves snacks made from organic food, from sweet to hearty. The wide choice of goodies makes it hard to decide. Finally, I chose both the **chocolate brownie** and the **tempeh sandwich**. I install myself with my loot on a bench in the sun. The tempeh is crunchy and the dressing of mustard and maple syrup elevates the sandwich to a higher level. The topping of jalapeño on the chocolate brownie is on first sight surprising. But already a thousand years ago, the Mayas made a drink out of chocolate and chili peppers.

I watch as the line in front of the Cinnamon Snail truck becomes longer and longer. Dozens of neatly dressed business men and women patiently wait their turn for a healthy lunch.

→ continues on p. 062

해초무침 Veg	콩나물 Veg	도라지무침 Veg	감자조림 Veg	미역+게맛살
Seasoned Seaweed	Beansprout	Bellflower Root	Potato	Seaweed + Crab

장어정식과 국 또는 샐러드	양념치킨
Eel Lunch Box (w/Soup or Salad)	Spicy Chicken

모둠나물	소고기찐만두	오이무침
	Steamed Beef Dumpling	Spicy

BULGOGI

Korean beef

STEP BY STEP!

\# Mix the soy sauce with the sugar, sesame oil, garlic, ginger and chili powder.

\# Rub the meat with the marinade and let rest for 1 hour.

\# Take the meat out of the marinade.

\# Heat the oil in a pot and fry the julienned onion to a golden brown. Add the chives and sesame seed and serve with rice.

INGREDIENTS

- ⅓ cup soy sauce
- 3 tbsp. sugar
- 2 tsp. sesame oil
- 2 cloves garlic, finely chopped
- ¼ tsp. fresh ginger, grated
- ⅛ tsp. chili powder
- 1 lb thinly sliced beef strips
- 2 tbsp. vegetable oil
- 1 small onion, julienned
- 2 chives, finely cut
- 2 tbsp. sesame seeds, roasted

* THERE'S MORE *

Bulgogi means literally 'fire meat'. Traditionally it is roasted on specially designed grills.

(L) — Manhattan: Midtown South

($)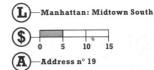

0   5   10   15

(A) — Address n° 19

Oh Happy day

INGREDIENTS

- 1 Chinese cabbage
- 5 tbsp. salt
- 1 tbsp. fish sauce
- 3 chives, cut in 1 inch pieces
- 1 small onion, finely chopped
- 2 cloves garlic, finely chopped
- 1 tbsp. sugar
- 1 tsp. fresh ginger, grated
- 2 tbsp. chili powder

I love kimchi
as a side dish
or as seasoning
in soups.

KIMCHI
Korean
fermented cabbage

Ⓛ —Manhattan: Midtown South

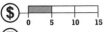

Ⓐ —Address n° 19

STEP BY STEP!

Slice the Chinese cabbage lengthwise in 2 halfs. Cut each half in 3 pieces, remove the hard end. Rinse the cabbage with water. Pat dry. Rub each leaf with salt. Layer the leaves in an oven dish. Let rest for 6 hours in the refrigerator to ferment. Kimchi can be stored in the fridge for several weeks, even months.

Rinse the cabbage well and press it to remove excess water. In a large bowl, combine cabbage with fish sauce, chives, onion, garlic, sugar and ginger, mix well. Rub with chili powder.

Place the cabbage in an airtight container and let rest to ferment for 4 days in a cool place.

Serve with rice dishes or use as a base in soup or wok dishes.

* THERE'S MORE *

According to some, this dish is more than 2500 years old and ranks among the five healthiest dishes in the world. The fermentation process produces vitamines A, B and C.

BROWNIE

Brownies are a pastry somewhere in between a cake and a cookie. The first recipe is said to have been conceived at the end of the 19th century by a chef at the luxury hotel Palmer in Chicago. They became very popular as a snack or dessert in the US and Canada. Today, there are many other countries where the American bar cookie is well liked.

* THERE'S MORE *

Brownies are sold all over New York. Because there are so many different recipes, quality and price can vary widely. A brownie is a simple, tasty dessert which can be given a festive note by serving it with a scoop of ice cream or by adding a cloud of unsweetened whipped cream and some raspberries or slices of strawberry.

INGREDIENTS

- 4 oz unsalted butter
- 8 oz semisweet chocolate
- 10 oz sugar
- 2 eggs
- 1 oz unsweetened cocoa
- ½ tsp. salt
- ⅓ cup flour
- oil to grease the baking pan

(L) —Manhattan: Midtown

($) | 0 | 5 | 10 | 15 |

(A) —Address n° 15

You can also add chile or nuts to the mixture.

STEP BY STEP!

Heat the oven to 350 °F.

Melt the butter and chocolate au bain- marie (place the chocolate in a heatproof bowl over a pan of simmering water. The base of the bowl should sit above the water without touching it). Stir with a metal spoon to make sure all pieces of chocolate are melted).

Remove the mixing bowl from the pot and add the sugar. Add the eggs one by one, stir. Add the unsweetened cocoa powder and salt, mix well. Add the flour and mix again. Grease an 8 inch square pan. Dust the surface with flour to avoid burning. Pour the batter into the pan.

Bake for 30 to 35 minutes. Check for doneness by inserting a toothpick into the center of the pan. If there are a few moist crumbs sticking on the toothpick then the brownies are ready. Brownies should be softer and have a bit more moisture then cake, so don't wait till the toothpick comes out dry.

Remove the brownies from the oven. Let cool for 15 minutes in the pan. Transfer to a rack for further cooling. Cut into 9 squares. Serve or keep in a tin or aluminum foil to prevent drying out.

INGREDIENTS

- 4 slices of bread
- 7 oz seitan
- 2 tbsp. vegetable oil
- ½ onion, sliced
- 1 tomato, sliced
- a handful of arugula
- 4 tbsp. Dijon mustard
- 2 tbsp. maple syrup
- pepper and salt

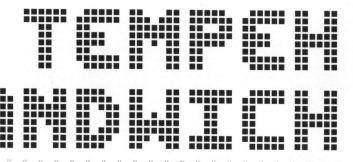

TEMPEH SANDWICH

A healthy in between snack. I tasted it for the first time at *The Cinnamon Snail*. This food truck is known for its healthy and original snacks.

STEP BY STEP!

Toast the bread.

Cut the seitan into ⅓ inch slices.

Add 2 tbsp. oil in a skillet and fry the seitan for 2 minutes on each side.

Whisk the Dijon mustard and maple syrup together. Season to taste with pepper and salt.

Brush the toast on one side with the mustard-maple syrup mix, add some arugula, a slice of tomato, a slice of seitan and a few onion rings. Put the second slice of toasted bread on top.

Cut diagonally and serve.

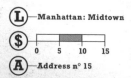

Ⓛ —Manhattan: Midtown

Ⓢ 0 5 10 15

Ⓐ —Address n° 15

It's a good idea to first marinate the seitan for a couple of hours in a marinade of, for example, a couple of tbsps. soy sauce and five-spice powder or soy sauce and lemon grass. Use your imagination.

This Week's special:
Porcini mushroom tempeh meatball sub
With garlic white bean puree
Red wine & basil tomato sauce
and marinated kale on a grilled baguette
$9.00

Make
Ma

8th
annual

VEN

OU

W

Cinn

STR

Lunch time in New York

Every working day around noon, an organized chaos erupts in New York. Millions of people are hungry. They want food! Now! Every day, a gigantic army of men and women stands ready to serve them. In ultra posh restaurants, old-fashioned diners, colorful salad- and sandwich bars, popular food stalls and gourmet food trucks. Tourists, immigrants and even seasoned New Yorkers like me are amazed by the size and the haste of the crowd. And by the enormous choice of food available to them. Would you like a **pastrami sandwich**? A plate of **pork meat with green sauce**, a bowl of **Manhattan clam chowder**, a fresh **ginger drink** or maybe a **smoothie**? Whatever you hanker for, you'll find it in New York.

The modern concept of 'lunch' was born in New York. Traditionally the meal around noon was the most important of the day, in America as well as in Europe. It was called 'dinner' while 'lunch' was the name for a snack in between, whether eaten during the day or in the evening. During the 19th century, the meal pattern began to change, under the pressure of industrialization. Nowhere was the change as radical as in New York. The biggest city of America was the bustling center of commerce, industry and finance. Workers and office clerks were allowed a limited time for their midday meal, often less than half an hour. So the elaborate meal (dinner) was only possible in the evening. Lunch became the name for what people ate between twelve and two pm.

Around 1900, New York had become a city where everything revolved around speed and efficiency. Pocket watches became widely used and time-clocks were introduced to control the arrival and departure times of employees. The most important thing about the lunch break was not the quality of the food but the amount of time needed to eat it. The term 'quick-lunch' became common in New York and spread from there through out the land. The term not only referred to the speedy meals but also to the restaurants specializing in them. The growing distance between homes and work places accelerated the trend. The commercial center of New York was situated in the lower half of Manhattan, but an increasing number of middle class people, merchants and bankers moved to the quieter neighborhoods uptown. It became unpractical for them to go home for their meals. Instead, they appeased their hunger in a quick-lunch so that they could go back to work in a jiffy.

In 1912 the New Yorkers Joe Horn and Frank Hardart introduced the first 'Automat', a concept that had existed in Europe since the 1880s. It was a splendid business with a facade of stained glass two stories high, marble floors and opulent sculpted ceilings, right in the middle of Times Square. New York embraced it instantly. More efficient was impossible. You slipped a nickel in a slot, opened a little door and pulled out a bowl of **coleslaw and potato salad** or a portion of **ham with pineapple** or a slice of **cheesecake**. It was a modern miracle. By the early 1930s New York had 41 of these Automats.

At their high point, every day they delivered fresh and cheap meals to 750.000 people from all walks of life. By the 1950s, their popularity waned because of competition from the new fast food joints and company cafeterias. Another problem was that the Automats accepted only coins of 5 and 25 cents. The last Automat closed in 1991. There are still New Yorkers who mourn this.

A more expensive form of lunching is the so-called 'power lunch.' The term was first used in the magazine Esquire in 1979, in an article about the Grill Room of the Four Seasons restaurant in New York. But the phenomenon itself is much older. Businessmen of a certain stature were not bound to limit their lunches to a mere half hour. They could take their time to eat out with colleagues and make deals while eating and drinking. The concept of a business lunch was launched by Delmonico's, an expensive restaurant in the Wall Street area. But the notion of a 'power lunch' is not limited to the business world. Other New

Yorkers too make lunch appointments to exchange ideas, make contacts, check out the competition and assure themselves that they still count.

But expensive restaurants are boring after a while. That's why business people too are lunching at food stands. Rich and poor, bankers and managers in expensive suits as well as construction workers and students, are lining up every day for the culinary wizards of the street. This is the real New York way. You eat your **bagel, rice with beans, grilled cheese sandwich** or **hot dog with onion sauce** standing up, walking or sitting in a square or park.

Every day, hundreds of thousands New Yorkers eat a free lunch. The kids of the public schools get, depending on the income of their parents, a free or very cheap lunch in school, including during vacations. The tradition started in 1908 in an elementary school near Times Square. Half a century later, all the public schools in the country had the obligation to offer lunch to their students. Then there are also many 'soup kitchens' where homeless people and others with a small or no pension can get a warm meal for free. Some are programs set up by the city but most are run by charities. Unfortunately, the lines of needy people get longer every year. More than once, all the food is gone before everyone is served and people have to be sent away hungry. That too, is part of reality in this city of incredible affluence.

This dish originated
in Rumania and spread
to the Jewish community.
In Rumania
it was usually made
with mutton.

The preparation of pastrami
is not without risks
for bacteria.
Because the pickling
of the meat takes 3 weeks,
it's important to work
very hygienically.
Make sure that the meat
remains submerged
all the time.

Add different spices for
different taste sensations.
Think of cinnamon, cumin,
ginger powder...

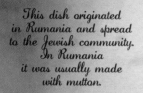

KATZ'S
DELICATESSEN

PASTRAMI
Smoked and pickled beef

★ ★

This reminds me of Joey from the sitcom *Friends* and of course of Katz's, the famous Jewish deli in Manhattan.

L—Manhattan: Lower East Side

$— 0 5 10 15

A—Address n° 23

INGREDIENTS

Marinade
- 1 gallon water
- 3 ½ oz salt
- 3 ½ oz sugar
- 2 tbsp. black pepper, ground
- 4 bay leaves
- 4 sprigs of fresh thyme
- 4 cloves garlic, mashed
- 1 tbsp. juniper berries
- 4 lbs beef

Garnish
- 2 tbsp. juniper berries
- 1 tbsp. coriander seeds
- 2 sprigs of fresh thyme
- 3 tbsp. whole black pepper

STEP BY STEP!

In a stockpot heat the gallon of water with the salt and sugar till completely dissolved. Turn off the heat, add black pepper, bay leaves, thyme, garlic and juniper berries. Let the herbs soak for about an hour.

Put the meat in a deep oven dish and pour the water-and-herb mixture over it. Cover with plastic wrap and put a weight on top to make sure the meat stays submerged. Turn the meat every couple of days for a total period of 20 days.

Pound the herbs for the garnish in a mortar till they have reached a coarse texture. Rub the meat with it on all sides.

Set up smoker or grill for smoking. Smoke the meat for about 3 hours.

Finally add some water to an oven dish and place the meat in it. Bake in a 250°F oven for 2 hours.
Let cool and cut into thin slices. Pastrami is delicious on sandwiches.

Nobody
seems to know
who made the first
clam chowder with tomatoes,
known today as Manhattan
clam chowder.
But already in the 1880s
the soup was popular in the
hotel-restaurants
of Coney Island,
Brighton Beach and
Manhattan Beach.
Later, after the extension
of the subway
to Coney Island in 1921
made the place
a mass-destination,
Manhattan clam chowder
became
a widely popular dish.

The origin of the word
chowder is also unsure.
It could be derived from
the word chaudière (kettle),
after the kettles used
by Breton fishermen
in Newfoundland
to make soup on the beach
with the catch of the day
and any other ingredients
near at hand.

Ⓛ —Manhattan: Chelsea

Ⓢ 0 5 10 15

Ⓐ —Address: Markets
& food courts G

MANHATTAN

CLAM

CHOWDER

Clam chowder is a thick
soup made with clams.
There are different versions,
depending on the region.
Best known are the New
England chowder, a white
version made with cream
or milk, and the Manhattan
clam chowder, the red
version made with tomatoes.

INGREDIENTS

- 3 cups water
- 3 ½ lbs quahog or large
  cherrystone clams (well-
  washed, discard the ones that
  are open)
- 2 slices of bacon, cut into
  ½ inch pieces.
- 1 onion, medium size, finely
  chopped
- 1 rib celery, diced
- ¼ red pepper, diced
- 1 carrot, diced
- 3 cloves garlic, finely
  chopped
- 2 bay leaves
- 1 tbsp. oregano
- 2 sprigs of fresh thyme
- a pinch of cayenne pepper
- ¾ lb potatoes, cubed
- ½ cup chicken stock
- 1 (oz) canned tomatoes,
  chopped
- half a bundle of parsley, finely
  chopped
- salt
- black pepper, freshly ground

Garnish
- saltine crackers

STEP BY STEP!

In a pot, bring 3 cups of water to a boil. Add the clams and
cover. Let cook for 5 minutes. Uncover, stir with wooden
spoon. Let cook for another 5 to 10 minutes depending on
the type and size of the clams or until most of the clams are
opened.
Remove the shells but save the broth. Strain the broth. Let
the clams cool and cut into ⅛ inch or smaller pieces. Set the
clams and broth aside the clam meat.

Cook the bacon in a pot and cook over medium- low heat
until golden brown. Add the onion, celery, red pepper and
carrot. Toss well, then cook over medium heat until the
vegetables are well wilted, about 10 minutes. Add garlic,
bay leaves, oregano, thyme and cayenne pepper, cook for
another 2 minutes.

Add the potatoes, the clam broth (you need about 3 cups
so add some water if necessary) and chicken stock. Bring to
a boil, then adjust heat so broth just simmers. Cover. Cook
until the potatoes are tender, about 15 to 20 minutes. Add the
tomatoes. Continue to simmer another 10 to 15 minutes.

Shut off the heat, add the chopped clams and parsley.
Season to taste with salt and pepper. Let the soup rest for
at least an hour, preferably longer. This will allow flavors to
blend. Gently reheat just to the simmering point.

Serve very hot.

The traditional way to serve Manhattan Clam Chowder is
with crumbled saltine crackers, small salted biscuits.

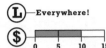

(L)—Everywhere!

($) 0 5 10 15

INGREDIENTS

- 2 cups spinach (or Coriander, mint or parsley)
- 1 ripe banana
- ¼ cup milk
- ¼ cup orange juice

STEP BY STEP!

Mix all ingredients in the blender until smooth.

For a refreshing summer drink add some ice cubes in the blender or before serving.

SMOOTHIE

A smoothie is a drink made with fresh vegetables and/or fruit and sometimes with milk, in a blender. It's a very popular drink which you can buy in the streets as well as in some stores and restaurants in New York. The great thing about smoothies is that there are as many kinds as there are personal tastes. Here is the basic recipe with which I like to start my day.

* THERE'S MORE *

The concept of the smoothie has existed for centuries. There are versions of it in the Mediterranean area, the Middle East, India, Central and South America.

COLE SLAW

'Kool slaa' is a culinary legacy of the Dutch colonial period of New York. Cole slaw, as it became known in English, has become a classic side dish with sandwiches and hamburgers. It's also always available in barbecue restaurants and stands, salad bars and the ready made dishes department of food stores. The original cole slaw was mixed with oil and vinegar, or butter and vinegar.

INGREDIENTS

- ½ cup heavy cream
- 1 tbsp. sugar (optional)
- 1 tbsp. vinegar
- 2 tbsp. butter
- 1 small (approximately 1 lb) white cabbage, shredded
- sea salt, white pepper and paprika powder to taste

STEP BY STEP!

In a bowl, mix cream, sugar and vinegar. Let rest.

Melt the butter in a pot with heavy bottom; add the cabbage, salt and pepper. Cover and let simmer over medium heat for 5 minutes. Stir every now and then. Strain the cabbage and transfer to a bowl.

Pour the cream over the cabbage, blend well. Sprinkle with paprika.

* THERE'S MORE *

The version of cole slaw with mayonnaise was introduced by German immigrants in de 19th century. Meanwhile, there are many variations of this dish. Some mix the cole slaw with carrots, green peppers and celery. Others add garlic, anchovy and bacon, or, to give it an Asian flavor, you can add fresh cilantro, garlic, scallions, dried shrimp, lemon and roasted sesame oil.

POTATO SALAD

★ ★

Potato salad is a popular basic dish in New York and the rest of the US. It's a standard item in every salad bar, deli, diner, soul food cafeteria and barbecue joint. It's seldom absent at summer picnics and buffets.

INGREDIENTS

- 1 tbsp. fresh basil, finely chopped
- 1 ½ tsp. fresh marjoram, finely chopped
- 1 ½ tsp. fresh thyme or/and savory
- ¼ cup mayonnaise
- ½ cup red onion, thinly sliced
- ¼ cup apple cider vinegar
- 4 cups cubed cooked potatoes (about 2 lbs)
- 2 eggs, hard boiled, cut in small pieces
- salt and freshly grounded black pepper to taste

STEP BY STEP!

\# In a small bowl, blend basil, marjoram, thyme and mayonnaise, cover and let rest in the refrigerator for about 2 hours.

\# In a separate small bowl, mix the onion and vinegar. Let rest for 15 minutes and strain.

\# Blend the potatoes, eggs, salt, pepper and onion. Add the mayonnaise mixture and gently toss. Serve immediately or keep in cool place.

Ⓛ —Everywhere!

Ⓢ | 0 | 5 | 10 | 15 |

THERE'S MORE

These days there are more than a thousand varieties of potatoes. At the Union Square Greenmarket you will find 20 to 30 kinds. You can make countless variations of potato salad by adding ingredients such as fresh parsley, dill, chervil, squares of apple, strips of fried smoked bacon or finely chopped celery. A salad of young, unpeeled potatoes looks pretty and fresh.

INGREDIENTS

- 1 (6 to 7 pound) fully cooked ham shoulder
- ¼ cup pineapple juice
- ¼ cup brown sugar
- ¼ cup honey
- 1 lb fresh pineapple slices or 1 can (15 ¼ oz)
- Maraschino cherries
- whole cloves

PINEAPPLE FLAVORED HAM

Ham is an important ingredient in the traditional cuisine of the southern US. There are many recipes. The salted meat is often combined with the sweet taste of pineapple, mango or apples. Ham is served at parties, picnics, Sunday family meals and in soul food restaurants.

STEP BY STEP!

\# Remove skin from ham; place ham, fat side up, on a baking rack or in a shallow pan. Cover ham loosely with aluminum foil. When using meat thermometer, make sure it does not touch fat or bone. Heat at 325 ˚F for 25 to 30 minutes per pound or until meat thermometer registers 140 ˚F.

\# Combine pineapple juice, brown sugar and honey in a heavy saucepan; cook over low heat until sugar dissolves, stirring often.

\# Remove foil; score fat in a diamond design. Brush ham with pineapple glaze. Arrange pineapple slices and cherries in desired pattern, securing with wooden picks; stud ham with cloves, and brush with glaze. Bake at 325 °F for an additional 25 to 30 minutes; baste with glaze. Place ham on serving plate with okra, tomatoes and plantains.

* THERE'S MORE *

According to the connoisseurs, the best cooked and smoked hams come from the state of Virginia. The sale of hams in the US peaks around Easter, Thanksgiving and Christmas.

Crust

- 1 vanilla bean
- 1 cup all-purpose flour
- ¼ cup sugar
- 1 egg yolk
- 8 tbsps. unsalted butter, cut into bits
- a pinch of salt

Filling

- 2 ½ pounds Philadelphia-cream cheese, at room temperature
- 1 ¾ cups sugar
- 3 tbsps. all- purpose flour
- 1 ½ tsp. freshly grated lemon zest
- 1 ½ tsp. freshly grated orange zest
- ½ tsp. vanilla extract
- 5 whole eggs
- 2 egg yolks
- ¼ cup heavy cream

CHEESE= CAKE

★ ★ ★ ★ ★ ★ ★ ★ ★ ★ ★ ★ ★ ★ ★ ★ ★ ★

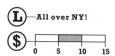

ⓛ —All over NY!

$ 0 5 10 15

The classic New York cheesecake is creamy and smooth, thick but not heavy. It's a richer version of the drier cheese pie recipes East-European immigrants brought with them. The New York version became widespread in the early 20th century. The cheesecake remains a very popular dessert.

MAKE THE CRUST:

Split the vanilla bean lengthwise, and scrape the seeds into a bowl. Stir in the flour, sugar and lemon zest. Mix with a whisk. Add the egg yolk, butter, salt and knead the mixture until it forms a smooth dough.

Flatten the dough into a ⅛ inch thick round, and chill it, wrapped in wax paper or aluminum foil, for 1 hour.

Preheat the oven to 400 °F.

Remove the sides of a 9 inch springform pan. Grease the bottom of the pan lightly, and cover it with enough dough to cover. Reserve the remaining dough. Bake the bottom crust in the middle of the pre-heated oven for 10 to 12 minutes.

Remove from the oven, let cool for 10 minutes, then chill it in the refrigerator for at least 30 minutes.
Grease the sides of the pan, reattach them to the bottom (the bottom that has the baked crust) and cover the sides with a ⅛ inch layer of the remaining dough. Set aside.

TO MAKE THE FILLING:

Preheat the oven to 550 °F.

In a stand mixer (or in a large bowl, using a hand-held mixer), beat the cream cheese with the sugar, the flour, the zests, and the vanilla until the mixture is smooth. Beat in the whole eggs and the egg yolks, one at the time, beating lightly after each addition. Stir in the cream.

Pour the filling into the springform with prepared crust and bake the cheesecake in the middle of the preheated oven for 12 minutes. Reduce the heat to 200 °F. Bake the cheesecake for 1 hour more.

Remove the cheesecake from the oven. Let cool in the pan on a rack. Still in the pan, chill for at least 8 hours. Remove the cake from the refrigerator about an hour before serving.

VARIATION:

The bottom crust can also be made with a layer of sponge cake or a crust of crumbled cookies or graham crackers. The cake can be covered with strawberry or pineapple slices. For a chocolate cheesecake, melted chocolate is added to the dough.

The most famous commercial cheesecake
is from Junior's, a well-known restaurant
in Brooklyn which opened in 1950.
In 1974 New York magazine proclaimed it the best
cheesecake of the city. Nowadays it's sold by mail
order all over the country. It's also sold on
Times Square and in the food court
in Grand Central Station.

In 1910 there were so many bagel bakeries in New York that a trade union of bagel bakers was formed. The profession was a 'closed shop': only sons and cousins of bagel bakers could become members of the union and get a job in a bagel bakery.

Bagels were made by hand until the early 1960s when Dan Thompson, a Canadian bagel baker, developed a machine which formed the dough rings and cooked the bagels.

BAGELS

///

(L) —Manhattan: Lower East Side

($) | 0   5   10   15 |

(A) —Address n° 21

INGREDIENTS

- 2 tsps. dry yeast
- 1 ½ tbsp. sugar
- 1 ¼ cups warm water
- 1 lb bread flour
- 1 ½ tsp. salt
- vegetable oil

The bagel was introduced in New York in the 19th century by East- European immigrants. Even then the recipe was already centuries old. At first, the New York bagels were much smaller than the big, inflated commercial dough rings that are sold today. If you want to buy a real, authentic, small fresh bagel, the kind that is first boiled and then baked, there is only one address in New York: Russ & Daughters, flourishing since 1914 on Houston Street in the Lower East Side.

Bagels are often served with cream cheese, smoked salmon and onion.

STEP BY STEP!

In a small bowl add yeast and sugar to ⅓ cup water. Don't stir. Wait 5 minutes, then stir until yeast and sugar are dissolved. Mix the flour and salt in a large bowl. Make a well in the middle and pour in the yeast and sugar mixture.

Pour half of the remaining water into the well. Mix. Depending on the weather and where you live, you may need to add anywhere from a couple of tbsps. to approximately 1 cup. Mix till you have a moist and firm dough. Knead the dough for about 10 minutes until it is smooth and elastic.

Grease a mixing bowl with vegetable oil and turn the dough to coat. Cover the dough with a damp kitchen towel. Let rise in a warm place for 1 hour, until the dough has doubled in size. Punch the dough down and let rest for another 10 minutes.

Carefully divide the dough into 8 equal pieces (you may want to use a kitchen scale). Shape each piece into a round. Now, take a dough ball and press it gently against the work surface, moving your hand and the ball in a circular motion pulling the dough into itself while reducing the pressure on top of the dough slightly, until a perfect dough ball forms. Repeat with the rest of the dough.

Coat a finger in flour and gently press your finger into the center of each dough ball to form a ring. Stretch the ring to about ⅓ diameter of the bagel and place on a lightly oiled cookie sheet. Repeat the same step with the remaining dough. Cover with a damp kitchen towel and let rest for 10 minutes.

Meanwhile, preheat the oven to 425 °F.

Bring a large pot of water to a boil. Reduce the heat. Lower the bagels into the water. Wait till the bagels float to the surface and then let them cook for at least 1 minute longer but no more than 2 minutes. Boil as many as you are comfortable with boiling. Place the bagels on the lightly oiled cookie sheet.

If you want to add toppings to the bagel, do so as you take them out of the water. First use egg wash to make the topping stick. Then you can sprinkle some coarse salt, finely chopped garlic or onion, sesame seeds or caraway seeds on the bagels.

Bake the bagels for 20 minutes, until golden brown. Let cool on a baking rack.

VARIATION

You can sprinkle the bagels with a topping of your choice: garlic or onion, sesame seeds or caraway seeds.

E WHEAT
YTHING
GRINDSTONE
BALTIC RY
CHALLAH
CHALLAH
RUSS & DAUGHTER

In an international city like New York there are of course huge quantities of rice consumed every day. 'Rice with beans' is a nutritious cheap dish which is an important part of the traditional diet in Latin America, the Caribbean islands and the South of the US.

RED BEANS AND RICE, LOUISIANA STYLE

★ ★

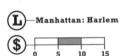
—Manhattan: Harlem

$ | 0 5 10 15 |

* THERE'S MORE *

Rice is, after grain, corn and potatoes, the most consumed form of starch in the world. The cultivation of rice in the US began in the 17th century. Today, it's grown in seven states: Arkansas, California, Texas, Louisiana, Mississippi, Missouri and Florida.

INGREDIENTS

- 1 lb dried small red beans, picked over and rinsed
- 6 cups water
- 1 large smoked ham hock
- 1 large onion, chopped
- 2 cloves garlic, minced
- ½ lb chopped beef
- 2 tbsp. parsley, finely chopped
- ½ tsp. red pepper
- salt to taste
- 3 bay leaves
- 4 cups cooked long grain white rice
- a few sprigs of parsley

STEP BY STEP!

In a heavy- bottomed pot soak the rinsed beans for 8 to 10 hours. Drain. Rinse again. Return to the pot. Add 6 cups of water, ham hock, onion and garlic. Bring to a boil and cook for 10 minutes.

Meantime cook the chopped beef. Drain the fat. Add the beef, parsley, red pepper, salt and bay leaves to the beans and simmer uncovered for 2 to 2½ hours.

Remove the ham hock and bay leaves. Let cool. Remove the fatty tissue and bone from the ham hock. Cut the meat in bite- size pieces and stir into the beans.

Serve over cooked rice. Garnish with fresh parsley.

GRILLED CHEESE & PORK SANDWICH

L—Manhattan: Midtown

$ 0 5 10 15

April is National Grilled Cheese Sandwich Month in America. This shows how popular this snack is. Traditionally, it's nothing more than two slices of factory- made white bread with some slices of melting cheese in between, usually eaten with tomato soup from a can. But for quite a while, the grilled cheese sandwich has outgrown this bland image. These days, every serious chef has his own recipe for this classic and in cities like New York, Los Angeles and Portland gourmet trucks do well with their own variations.

INGREDIENTS

- 4 tbsp. creamy butter
- 8 slices of good quality bread like sour dough, ciabatta or brioche
- 10 oz cheddar or gruyere, cut into thin slices
- ½ lb pulled pork

STEP BY STEP!

Butter four bread slices on one side.

Melt 1 tbsp. butter in a heavy-bottomed pan. Place each slice of buttered bread, butter side down in the pan. Cover with pulled pork and cheese. Let cook for about 5 minutes over medium heat. Don't press.

Cover with the remaining slices of bread; buttered side up. Carefully turn with spatula. Let cook for another 3 to 4 minutes. Lower the heat, making sure the cheese melts but the bread doesn't burn.

A grilled cheese sandwich can also be made in a sandwich press (panini-press) or open-faced under an oven-grill. Olive oil can be used instead of butter.

Other cheeses, such as mozzarella and brie, can be delectable alternatives, as long as their texture remains creamy when they melt. Meat lovers can add smoked bacon or ham to the cheese. You can also serve it with a fried egg. Slices of tomato and eggplant also fit well. The dish invites experimentation.

The boys and girls of the Milk Truck in New York generously butter the slices on both sides and grill the sandwiches in a panini-press. The guys of the Food Freaks truck spread mayonnaise on the outside of the bread. Mayonnaise burns less quickly than butter, which means that the bread can become more crunchy and the cheese more melted.

HOT DOG
ONION SAUCE

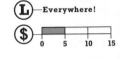

L —Everywhere!

$ | 0 5 10 15

For almost a century and a half, hot dogs have been associated with New York. Originally they were sold only with mustard and sauerkraut. Later – nobody seems to know exactly when – a sauce of onions and tomato was added. Every vendor used to make his own sauce. Nowadays different versions are sold in every supermarket. Fortunately, the new generation of food trucks has picked up the tradition of homemade sauces. The hot dogs on which they are poured usually are of a better quality too. What follows is a slight variation of the personal recipe of New York food expert Arthur Schwartz.

The hot dog was launched around 1870 in Coney Island in Brooklyn by an enterprising German immigrant, Charles Feltman.

INGREDIENTS

- 1 tbsp. olive oil
- 3 large sweet onions (about 2 ½ pounds) cut into ¼ inch dice or thinly sliced
- ¾ cup ready made chili sauce
- 12 oz tomato juice, fresh or canned
- 1 tsp. paprika powder
- ¼ tsp. dried oregano
- salt to taste
- ⅛ tsp. Tabasco sauce or to taste (or hot red pepper flakes)

STEP BY STEP!

In a sauce pan, heat the oil, add the onions and sauté for 10 to 15 minutes over medium heat, stirring constantly.

When the onions are well wilted, but not browned, add the remaining ingredients and stir to combine. Let simmer, partially covered, for about 30 minutes.

Season the sauce to taste with salt and Tabasco sauce or hot red pepper flakes. If using hot red pepper flakes, let simmer for a few minutes.

By the 1920s millions of them were sold every year in a gigantic Biergarten, the Ocean Pavilion, which Feltman had constructed at the shore. One of his employees, Nathan Handwerker, decided in 1916 to start his own hot dog business. Feltman' went bankrupt in 1946, but Nathan's in Coney Island is still besieged every summer by hundreds of thousands of hot dog lovers. Meanwhile, many hot dog vendors in New York are selling Nathan's hot dogs as well. They're also in most supermarkets. Since the 1930s Papaya King has sold a uniquely New Yorkish combination: a hot dog with a glass of fresh papaya juice.

The 'luxocratic' food trucks

By the end of the first decade of the 21st century food trucks became wildly popular in New York, and in other American cities too. One reason was the bad economy. Many consumers had to live more frugally, so they spent less on eating out. Also, many who dreamed of a culinary career had to lower their ambitions. The banks were no longer willing to loan them the money to start their own restaurant. But with the help of family, friends, credit cards and sites as Kick Start they could scrape enough money together to buy an old truck and convert it into a kitchen on wheels.

America is a society that is constantly moving. New York, even more so. A quick snack 'on the go' is part of daily life. But the typical New York street consumer of the 21st century does not only want to be served quickly, he also wants great tasting food that has been expertly prepared. The magazine Food&Wine calls the trend 'luxocratic,' a clever contraction of luxurious and democratic.

Food trucks have existed for a long time in New York but the phenomenon of the gourmet food trucks is relatively new. It began in the 1990s when there was a peak in immigration from Latin America. For many newcomers, the first stop was California, especially metropolitan Los Angeles. Enterprising immigrants began operating taco trucks. They drove them to construction sites, factories and other workplaces to provide cheap meals with the tastes of home to the immigrant workers. The long lines at the trucks attracted Americans and the word-of-mouth advertising about the savory, fresh and very cheap food spread quickly. The more immigrants arrived from the South, the more familiar a sight the taco truck became in the American urban landscape. They became a source of inspiration for a new wave of young chef-entrepreneurs with a nose for niche markets.

Cities like Los Angeles, San Francisco, Portland, Austin, Seattle, Saint Louis, Tampa, Washington D.C. and New York now all have a wide offering of food trucks specializing in ethnic food and fusion dishes. Every city has its own regulations. Chicago has the reputation of being the least food truck friendly. New York, the largest and most diversified city of the country, has the largest number of food trucks.

The food trucks have become part and parcel of the urban environment. They are so well integrated that more and more companies and others use them to cater parties and receptions. They even star in two television shows: The Great Food Truck Race (Food Network) and Eat Street (The Cooking Channel).

The popular Zagat guide created the website Foodtruck.Zagat.com in 2010 where consumers can look up food trucks according to location, cuisine and points given by the public.
Several organizations in New York offer walking and tasting tours of the food trucks: New York Street Food Walking Tours (Tours@newyorkstreetfood.com), New York Food Truck & Cart Walking Tour (info@sidewalksofny.com), Urban Oyster Food Cart Tour (urbanoyster. com).

→ continuation of p. 018

Across the street, Vivian of the Palenque Homemade Colombian food truck just puts her billboard out. I take a look at the menu and notice they have **arepas**. Arepas are corn pancakes with a topping of meat or vegetables with salsa. Vivian's eyes light up when I tell her that I visited Cartagena and Santa Marta in her country and got to know that delicious national dish. Proudly she tells me her recipe and the different variations she makes, some with sesame seeds and quinoa. She tells me she used to work for a fashion designer in Bogota. She gives me a **cocotta**, a goody made of sugar cane, ginger and coconut pulp. Very sweet but delicious.

47th Street is also the usual location of the Chinese Mirch truck and the Japanse Okadaman truck. Mirch sells **momo's**, Tibetan dumplings. Okadaman's specialty is **okonomiyaki**, the typical pancake of Osaka. The Czech New Yorker Jan Albert discovered this dish when he was traveling with his family in Osaka. Because the taste enchanted him and he had never seen it in New York, he got the idea to start a food truck. It caught on. The hearty pancake, the ingredients of which he imports from Japan, is becoming trendy **on** the streets of New York.

Entirely satisfied and still in the afterglow of my conversations with cheerful Vivian and enterprising Jan, I walk north to Má Pêche restaurant on 56th Street for a lecture on street food in New York. Near Park Avenue and 53rd Street I come across the King of Falafel. About twenty people are standing in line. The winsome chef rewards them with **falafel balls**, which are excellent to still the first hunger pangs. I join the line and buy one with **tahini sauce**. Tahini is a spread from the Middle East. King of Falafel began with a store in Astoria in Queens and is now a fixture of the New York midtown lunch scene. It delivers constant quality and the better kind of pita and falafel.

When I arrive in Má Pêche restaurant, the lecture has just started. We are treated to a well documented trip through the history of street food in New York and are offered a vision for the future. Oysters were a popular street food, as were warm corn cobs, **knishes**, and pickles. In Má Pêche I meet passionate people like Robert La Valave, the animator of the New Amsterdam Market. This is a splendid initiative. Local producers come together on Sundays in downtown Manhattan on the site where the legendary Fulton fish market used to be. They hawk their wares in a unique setting with a spectacular view of the Brooklyn Bridge. In Má Pêche I also meet the culinary journalist Jamie Feldmar who is on the verge of leaving for Thailand. I give her some travel tips and she in turn gives me the contact information of Jeff Orlick, a guy from Queens who is supposed to know the street food scene in Jackson Heights like no one else. His website is www.iwantmorefood.com. Just the kind of guy I want to meet.

After just two days in New York I'm already convinced: the street food scene of this city will never let go of me. In my head, vague plans for new street food adventures, and a book about them, are emerging. Back in my modest room, without taking off my coat, I send an email to Jacqueline Goossens, a journalist from my home country who **has** lived in New York since 1980. If there's somebody who needs to know about my street food plans, and who might be able to help me, it is she. We agree to meet the next day on a terrace in the *financial district*. She's enthusiastic about my plans and has even already arranged a meeting with Sean Basinski, a one time street vendor who is now a lawyer and the driving force behind the Street Vendors Projects and the Vendy Awards. With these initiatives, he defends the social and economic rights of the street vendors. Sean tells us how every day thousands of them, legally here or not, put their souls into preparing the most diverse dishes and make a living that way. The city does not always make things easy for them; it's difficult to obtain a license and the fines are high. 'Start spreading the news, we're making a book,' I think, while saying goodbye to Sean and Jacqueline and thanking them for sharing their passion for New York's culinary street life with me.

I want to spend my few remaining days as much as possible on the streets, to take in as many street food impressions as I can. In New York the fixed-gear bike is an often seen part of the streetscape, while in my home city, this trend is just emerging. Since I'm not insensitive to trends, I decide to rent one in a bike store in Alphabet City. Despite the speed and efficiency of the subway system, I prefer to get to know New York above ground. Equipped with a helmet and a lock that is heavier than the bike itself, I'm ready to cruise New York in search of more street food.

On a bike trip along the East River in Williamsburg on Sunday, fortuitously I find the Smorgasbord foodmarket. On an empty lot, under party tents and parasols, about forty food stalls offer all the ingredients for a fantastic feast. Most customers are young people, meeting each other and eating together on their day off. The atmosphere is very laid back. The market offers a wide variety of dishes from Latin America to India and Japan. You can enjoy oysters, donuts, grilled meats, fish & chips and much more. In one stall, the **bruschetta melanzane alla parmigiana** presented on a bruschetta catches my attention. I made this dish countless times for friends as a cold appetizer on a balmy summer night. Several layers of eggplant, **tomato sauce**, Parmesan cheese and a bit of freshly picked basil. The power of simplicity and quality ingredients is always very pronounced in Italian cuisine. I chat with the friendly salespeople who spontaneously tell me the secret of their **tomato sauce**. Another discovery on my Sunday brunch trip is the Salvadorian snack **pupusa**, fried dough filled with cheese and loroco, a flower which reminds me of cauliflower.

Back on my bike, I follow the East River upstream, direction Astoria. Once in a while I stop to admire the huge graffiti. I ride under the Queensboro Bridge. Kids play baseball in the eponymous park. My destination is the museum of the Japanese American sculptor Noguchi. After a relaxing visit, I bike, just for the kick, over the Queensboro Bridge to Manhattan. Before I even realize it, I'm in Central Park from which I cross to the Upper West Side, where I glide through 9th Avenue to Hell's Kitchen and further downtown. I make a quick visit to the posh Chelsea Market and then I cross Greenwich Village and Chinatown and ride over the Brooklyn Bridge to Williamsburg. Home sweet home. But mainly: New York by bike, what a kick! I highly recommend biking in New York. It allows you to get to know the city in a different way; you smell and hear everything, you stop where and when you want. With more than 200 kilometers of bike paths, New York has a surprisingly extensive biking infrastructure. Not everybody may agree but I think it's quite safe to bike in New York.

→ continues on p. 100

AREPA

COLOMBIAN PANCAKE

Ⓛ —Manhattan: Midtown

Ⓢ 0 5 10 15

Ⓐ —Address n°13

Palenque home made Colombian food and its owner Viviana
serve this snack with love...

INGREDIENTS

Beef
- ½ lb beef strips
- 2 cloves garlic, finely minced
- 1 onion, chopped
- 1 chive, finely minced
- ¼ tsp. cumin
- ¼ cup beer
- ¼ tsp. salt
- ¼ tsp. pepper
- 2 tbsp. vegetable oil

Arepa
- 1 lb cornmeal
- 1 tsp. salt
- 2½ cups warm water
- 2 tbsp. butter
- vegetable oil

Tomato salsa
- 2 tbsp. vegetable oil
- 1 onion, chopped
- 1 red chili pepper, jalepeno
- 1 lb fresh tomatoes, cored
- 2 cloves of garlic, mashed

- 1 handful fresh cilantro,
  chopped
- 2 tbsp. olive oil
- ¼ tsp. salt
- ¼ tsp. pepper
- juice of ½ lime
- olive oil

Garnish
- cooked beef strips
- ½ lb cotija cheese
- tomato salsa
- 1 handful of arugula

STEP BY STEP!

Start with the beef. Marinate the beef strips
in the onions, garlic, chive, cumin, beer, salt
and pepper. Let rest for 3 hours.

For the arepas:
In a bowl, sift the cornmeal, add the salt and
mix. Add water and mix in the butter. Cover
the bowl with plastic wrap. Let rest at room
temperature for 30 minutes.

Form about 20 small balls of dough. Use a
rolling pin to flatten the balls to disks of about
4 inches wide and ½ inch thick.

Add a tbsp. of vegetable oil to a heavy
skillet. Bake the arepa approximately for 5
minutes or until it's light brown, turn over and
bake for 5 more minutes.

For the tomato salsa: add 2 tbsp. of
vegetable oil in a pot over low heat. Add the
onions and cook until translucent and soft
but not brown. Add the jalapeño. Stir briefly.
Add the tomatoes, cook on medium. Add the
mashed garlic and chopped cilantro. Cook
sauce for about 1 hour over low. Add salt,
pepper, lime juice and olive oil according to
taste.

Remove beef from marinade and pat dry.
Cook the meat in 2 tbsp. of vegetable oil for a
few minutes till done.

Assembling the arepa. Scoop 2 tbsp. of meat
on the arepa, sprinkle 1 tbsp. of crumbled
cotija cheese on top and drizzle with a tbsp. of
the tomato salsa. Garnish with some arugula.

There are many resemblances
with the Mexican gordita and the
Salvadorian pupusa (see p 84).
Arepas are also a mainstay in Puerto Rico,
the Dominican Republic and Venezuela.
The Venezolan arepa is thicker than
the Colombian.

Worship
Everything.

COCOTTA

a Colombian sweet

This sweet snack looks like a small ball of knitting wool.

(L)—Manhattan: Midtown

($)
0   5   10   15

(A)—Address n° 13

INGREDIENTS

- 1 ¾ cups water
- 1 lb sugar
- zest of 1 lime
- 1 tbsp. fresh ginger, grated
- 1 tbsp. cinnamon powder
- 1 ¾ lb grated coconut

* THERE'S MORE *

There are many variations, depending on the cook and the region.

STEP BY STEP!

In a pot, add the water, cane sugar, lime zest, ginger and cinnamon. Heat till the sugar is completely dissolved and the mixture takes on a light caramel color.

Add the grated coconut a little bit at the time. Mix carefully with the caramel. Turn off the heat, and work quickly now, using a spoon to scoop up some of the mixture, make little balls of it and drop them on baking paper and repeat.

TIBETAN DUMPLINGS
(Momos)

★ ★

I tasted this for the first time in Pushkar, Rajasthan (India). In the northern part of India and in Nepal it's a popular street food snack. In New York I tasted it on Park Avenue, where many food trucks gather for the midtown lunch.

INGREDIENTS

The filling:
- 1 lb Chinese cabbage, finely shredded
- 1 lb mashed tofu
- salt
- 4 oz shiitake mushrooms
- 2 onions, finely chopped
- 2 inch piece of fresh ginger, grated
- 2 cloves garlic, finely chopped
- 1 handful fresh cilantro, finely chopped
- ½ tsp. white pepper
- 2 tbsp. soy sauce

For the dumplings
- 50 dumpling skins
- chili sauce
- salt

STEP BY STEP!

\# Sprinkle salt over the Chinese cabbage. Let rest for 15 minutes. Rinse well and squeeze to remove excess water.

\# Soak the shiitake in water for 20 minutes, drain, discard the hard edges of the mushrooms and chop finely. In a bowl, mix all ingredients well. Cover, refrigerate for 30 minutes.

\# Take a dumpling skin and place 1 tsp. of the filling in the middle of the dumpling. Fold the lower half of the dumpling over the filling. Now fold the upper half of the dumpling over the lower half and close, using a little bit of water. Repeat for all the dumplings.

\# In a steamer bring water to a boil. Steam dumplings for 10 minutes.

\# Serve with chili sauce.

* THERE'S MORE *
- - - - - - - - - - - - - - - - -

In China these steamed dumplings are called jiaozi, in Japan gyoza, although the latter are often first fried and then steamed. Jiaozi sometimes are cooked first.

Ⓛ —Manhattan: Midtown

$ ⬚ 0 5 10 15

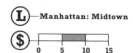

CAN'T WAIT TO GET
Mirch'd?

Tibetan Momos

5 handrolled, pan fried dumpling
served with your choice of hot o
sweet dipping sauce

Start Here: ➡

Vegetable:
The vegan choice - carrot, potato, cabbage minced with our secret spice

Chicken:
Infused with chopped ginger and cilantro

Keema:
Traditional Indian minced lamb & peas stir fry

Spinach:
With an equal dose of delicious white cheese

WHY NOT MAKE IT A:

Rice Bowl
Manchurian sauce or Garlic sauce
Served with momos, choice of long grain
basmati or brown rice & vegetables
$9/$10

Thukpa
Hearty and healthy
momos & noodle stew
$9/$10

Sliders
3 traditional baos with protein
filling & sauce of the month

Thirsty?
Mango Lassi
Our signature yogurt drink
billions of probiotic cultur

Dessert

OKONOMIYAKI

★ ★

PANCAKE FROM OSAKA

INGREDIENTS

- 10 oz Chinese cabbage,
  finely chopped
- 1 tsp. salt
- 3 ½ oz okonomiyaki flour
- 2/3 cup dashi bouillon
- 1 tbsp. white miso paste
- 1 tbsp. mirin, a kind of rice wine
- 2 large eggs, slightly
  beaten
- 3 chives, finely chopped
- 8 shiitake
- 4 slices bacon 4 inch each
  or 5 oz of seafood (shrimp,
  calamari...)
- pepper and salt
- 1 tbsp. vegetable oil

Sauce
- 3 tbsp. ketchup
- 2 tbsp. Japanese soy sauce
- 1 tbsp. sake
- 1 tbsp. mirin
- 1 tbsp. brown sugar
- 2 tbsp. rice vinegar
- 1 tsp. fresh ginger, grated
- 1 clove garlic, mashed
- ¼ tsp. Japanese mustard
- 2 tbsp. water

Garnish
- Japanese mayonnaise
- Aonori (seaweed flakes)
- katsuobushi (dried bonito/
  tuna flakes)

A pretty name for a pancake! Thanks to Jamie Feldmar
in New York I discovered this dish.

STEP BY STEP!

\# Cut the cabbage leaves in fine sections and sprinkle
with salt. Let rest for 10 minutes, rinse under cold water
and squeeze out the liquid.

\# Prepare the okonomiyaki sauce: add all sauce
ingredients in a saucepan and bring to a boil over low
heat. Let thicken for about 10 minutes, set apart.

\# In a bowl, sift the flour. In a second bowl, mix the dashi
with the miso paste and mirin into a smooth sauce. Make a
well in the flour, add the eggs and dashi- miso blend. Mix
well. Add chives, Chinese cabbage, shiitake and bacon
(or seafood), mix again. Season to taste with pepper and
salt.

\# Heat a pan over medium heat, add vegetable oil. Add
one fourth of the batter. Bake for about 5 minutes over low
heat. Place a plate on top of the pan and flip. Add pancake
carefully back to the pan and bake the other side for
another 5 minutes.

\# Serve on a plate. Drizzle the okonomiyaka sauce on top
of the pancake. Garnish with mayonnaise, seaweed and
bonito flakes.

* THERE'S MORE *

*Okonomiyaki flour is made of
nagaimo or taro root, a very starch-
rich plant. If you can't find any
okonomiyaki flour, try this dish with
1/5 potato starch and 4/5 ordinary
flour, with half a teaspoon of baking
powder added.*

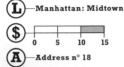

(L) —Manhattan: Midtown

($) 0 5 10 15

(A) —Address n° 18

INGREDIENTS

- 1 cup dried garbanzo beans (chickpeas), soaked overnight (or at least 8 hours) in cold water
- 1 onion, finely chopped
- 1 clove garlic, finely chopped
- 1 handful Italian (flat-leaf) parsley, finely chopped
- 1 handful fresh cilantro, finely chopped
- 1 tsp. coriander powder, finely ground
- 1 tsp. cumin powder
- ½ tsp. kurkuma
- 2 tbsp. flour
- pepper and salt to taste
- frying oil

Tahini sauce
- 5 tbsp. tahini paste
- ⅓ cup water
- 1 lemon
- ½ tbsp. salt

Serve with
- pita bread
- lettuce
- tomato
- onion
- red onion
- pickles

FALAFEL AND TAHINI SAUCE

Ⓛ —Manhattan: Midtow
$ | 0 5 10 15
Ⓐ —Address n° 16

>>

Fried chickenpea balls!

An Egyptian taxicab driver explained this recipe meticulously while we were on our way to the airport.

STEP BY STEP!

Drain the chickpeas. Smooth to puree in the blender or food processor.

Add onion, garlic, parsley, cilantro, coriander, cumin, curcuma and flour. Season to taste with pepper and salt.

Roll into balls of approximately 1 inch diameter. Fry in hot oil till golden brown.

Tahini sauce: in a bowl mix the tahini with water and lemon juice. Season to taste with salt.

Serve with pita bread, lettuce, tomato, onion, pickles and tahini sauce.

In 1921 New Yorkers Elia en Bella Gabay launched the deep-fried knish. Its advantage was that it could be easily transported and reheated. Knishes quickly became one of the most popular street food snacks.

After the second world war, knishes and hot dogs were often sold at the same stands. In the middle of the 1990s this was prohibited by the then mayor Giuliani, supposedly because it was unhygienic.

Quite a few New Yorkers regretted this. The combination of a hot dog and a knish, both lathered with mustard, was a cheap and substantial meal on the go.

KNISHES

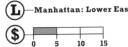

★ ★

Knishes are a kind of baked dumplings. They were introduced in New York in the 19th century by East- European immigrants. The classic New York knish is filled with potato and buckwheat. Nowadays there are also versions with vegetables like broccoli and spinach, usually mixed with potato.

INGREDIENTS

For the potato filling
- 2 ½ lbs Russet (baking) potatoes
- 2 tsp. salt
- a pinch of black pepper, freshly ground
- ¼ cup vegetable oil of rendered chicken fat
- 1 large onion, coarsely chopped

For the dough
- ¼ cup hot water
- 1 egg
- 1 tsp. salt
- ¼ tsp. black pepper, freshly ground
- 1. ½ cups flour
- 1 tsp. baking powder

For the egg wash
- 1 egg
- 2 tbsp. water

STEP BY STEP!

POTATO FILLING:
Cut the potatoes into chunks. Place them in a pot, cover with cold water, and bring to a boil. Drain immediately.

Using a food mill with the medium blade or a ricer (do not use a food processor), work the potatoes into a smooth puree. Add 1½ tsp. salt and pepper.

In a skillet, heat the oil. When the oil is hot but not smoking, add the onion. Fry until the onions are well wilted and begin to brown, stirring regularly. Add the remaining ½ tsp. salt.

Stir the onions into the mashed potatoes. Taste, and adjust the seasoning with salt and pepper. Cover and refrigerate until chilled.

DOUGH:
In the bowl of food processor or mixing bowl add water, egg, salt and pepper. Mix briefly. Add the flour and baking powder. Mix again until the dough is smooth.

Dust a work surface with some flour, and scrape the dough onto the surface. Knead the dough briefly, a minute or so. Wrap the dough in wax paper or plastic, and let it rest at room temperature for an hour.

KNISHES:
Preheat the oven to 375 °F. Cut the dough into two pieces. Roll out one piece at the time to a rectangle about 18 inches long and 8 inches wide. The long side of the dough should be facing you.

Take half of the potato mixture in your hand and make a long roll about 2 inches in diameter and 18 inch long. Put the roll on top of the dough, about 2 inches from the bottom edge.

Bring the bottom edge of the dough over the potato roll and brush the upper edge with egg. Bring the upper edge of the dough over the egg- washed edge.
Transfer the roll to a lightly greased baking sheet, seam down.
Repeat this with the other half of the dough and potato filling.

Once both rolls are on the baking sheet, carefully cut the roll into 2 inch pieces without cutting all the way to the baking sheet. Once the knishes are baked they will easily come apart.

Brush the logs with the egg wash.
Bake until golden, about 45 minutes.

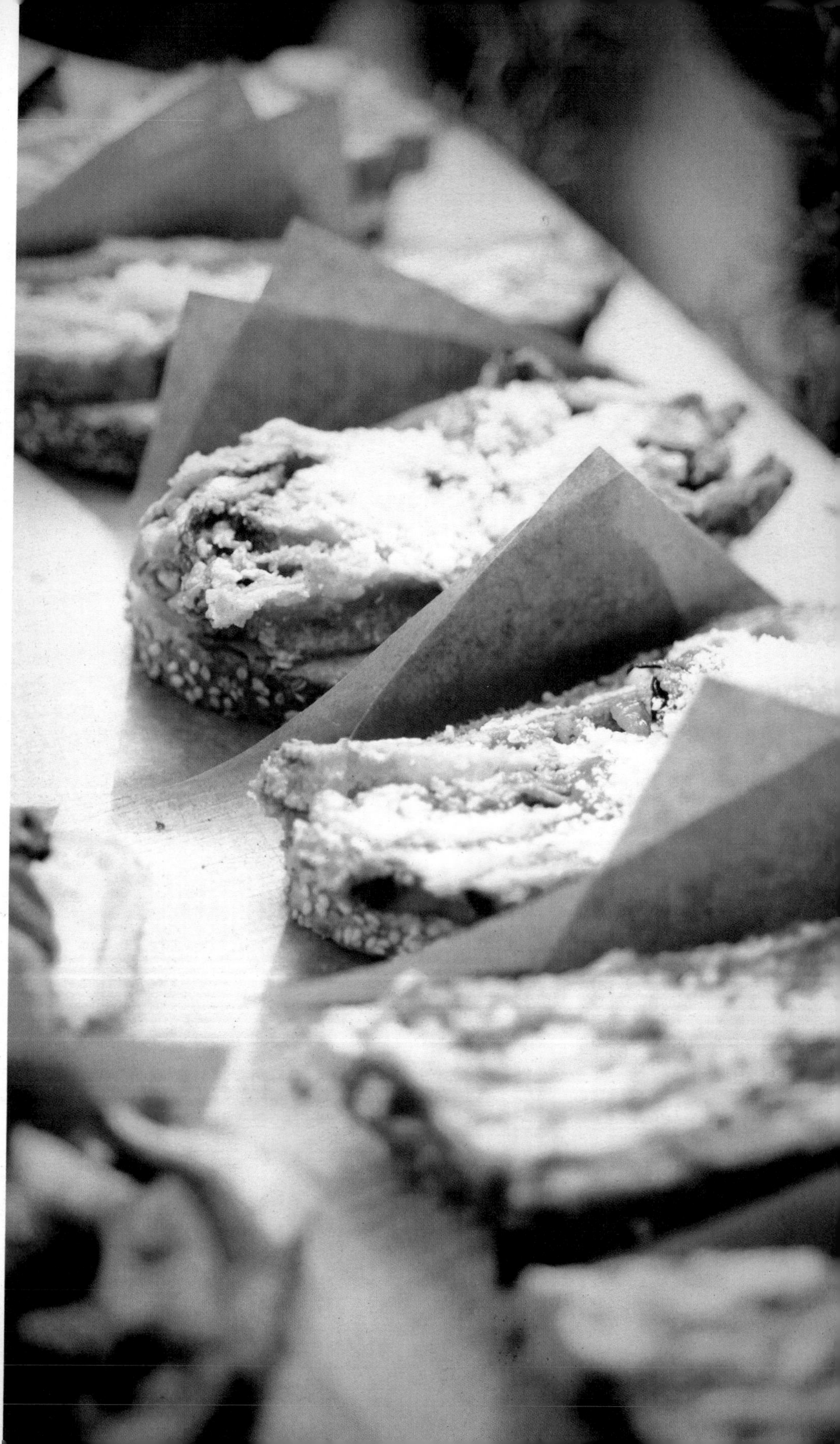

BRUSCHETTA MELANZANE
ALLA PARMIGIANA

Bruschetta with eggplant and parmezan cheese

This is a delicious dish to eat cold
on a balmy summer evening.

INGREDIENTS

- 2 lbs eggplant
- 1 tbsp. salt
- frying oil
- 2 lbs fresh tomatoes
  (or passata di pomodoro)
- 2 cloves of garlic, mashed
- 6 oz parmesan cheese, grated
- 1 handful fresh basil leaves
- ciabatta bread, cut in thick slices
  (about 1 inch), grilled to a crisp in
  the oven

Ⓛ —Brooklyn: Smorgasburg

Ⓢ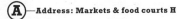

0   5   10   15

Ⓐ —Address: Markets & food courts H

STEP BY STEP!

Rinse the eggplants and cut in slices.
Put them in a sieve and sprinkle with salt.
Let rest for an hour. Rinse with water.
Pat dry with paper towels.

Heat the frying oil and fry the eggplant
till lightly browned. Arrange on a plate with
paper towels between the layers to absorb the
excess oil.

Prepare the tomato sauce. Let the tomatoes
simmer over a low flame until thickened.
Add salt, pepper and garlic. Take out the
garlic when the sauce is ready.

Arrange a layer of eggplant on a serving
dish. Pour tomato sauce on top. Add a thin
layer of parmesan cheese. Arrange basil
leaves on top. Repeat.
Put the dish in the refrigerator.

Cut in pieces of approximately 2 by 4 inches
and serve on crisply grilled ciabatta.

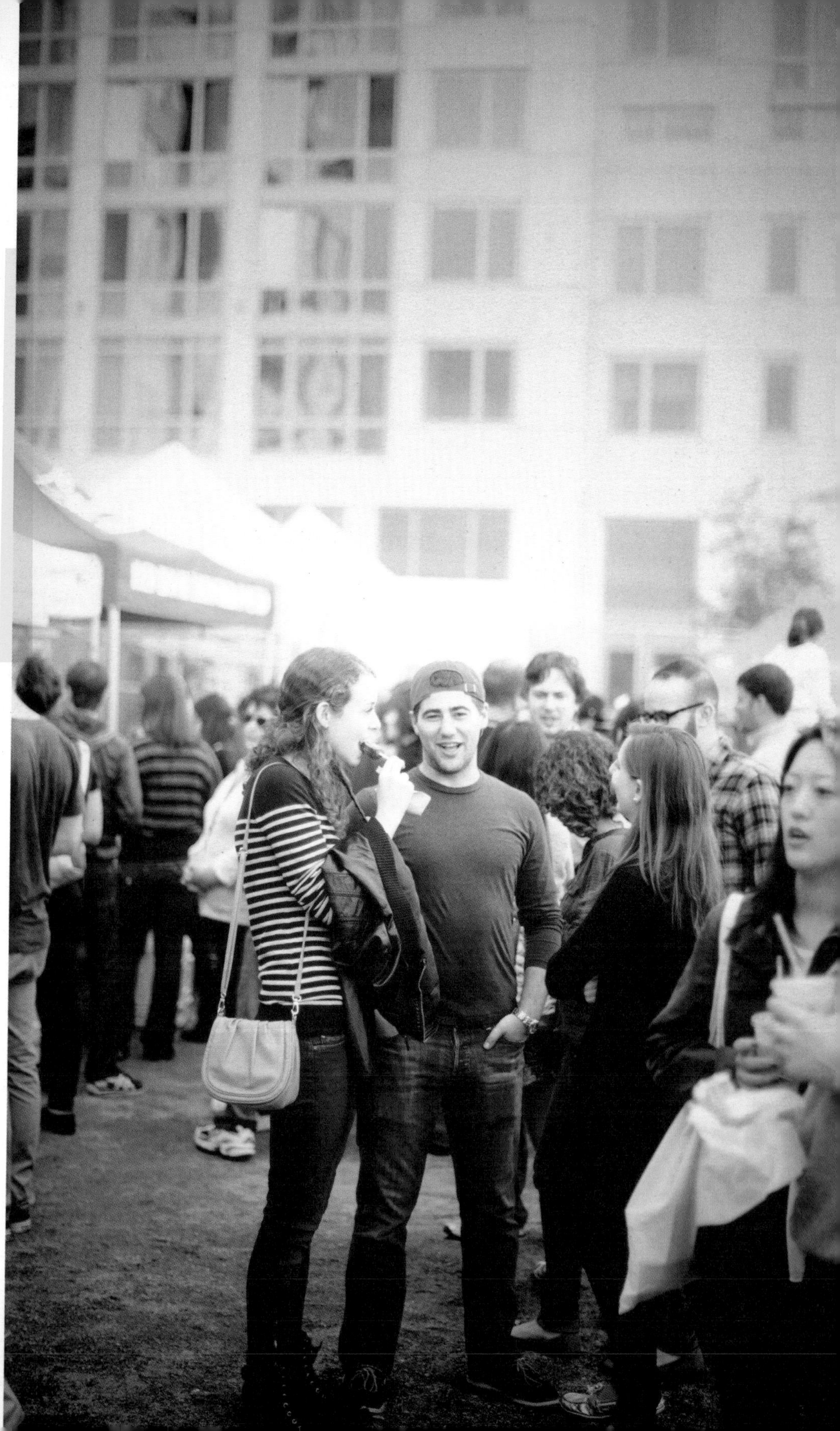

INGREDIENTS

- 4 ripe tomatoes, peeled and seeded if desired, chopped
- 2 tbsp. olive oil
- 1 small onion, finely chopped
- 2 cloves garlic, finely chopped
- sea salt and freshly ground black pepper to taste
- 1 or 2 tbsp. fresh basil, finely chopped

TOMATO SAUCE

The summers of New York are perfect for growing sun- ripened tomatoes. City dwellers plant them on terraces, roofs, private and community gardens and urban farms. Every summer you can buy locally grown tomatoes in open air markets and stores. Nothing goes better on a quality pasta than a simple sauce of fresh tomatoes.

 Ⓛ—Brooklyn: Smorgasburg

 Ⓢ

 0   5   10   15

Ⓐ—Address: Markets & food courts H

STEP BY STEP!

\# In a pan, heat oil over medium-high, add the onion. Cook, stirring frequently, until onion is soft, 4 to 5 minutes. Add the garlic, cook for another 2 minutes while stirring with a wooden spoon. Add tomatoes and cook over medium-low for about 5 minutes, stirring every now and then. Season to taste with salt and pepper. Turn off the heat. Scatter basil over the sauce.

✴ THERE'S MORE ✴

A 'red sauce restaurant' is the New York name for an eatery where most dishes are drenched in thick tomato sauce which has stewed on low heat for hours. Connoisseurs of the Italian culinary traditions call Little Italy the red sauce district. It's not meant as a compliment.

In that same Little Italy there are two yearly festivals, the feast of San Antonio in June and the feast of San Gennaro in September. Both have a huge offering of street food. Expect packed crowds, stands with games, and mountains of food, including tomato sauce.

PUPUSA

★ ★ ★ ★ ★ ★ ★ ★ ★ ★ ★ *Salvadorian pancake* ★ ★ ★ ★ ★ ★ ★ ★ ★ ★ ★ ★

I first tasted this nutritious snack at the Red Hook Ball Fields.

STEP BY STEP!

In a food processor or blender mix loroco flour and cheese well.
In a bowl mix the white cabbage with the grated carrot and jalapeño pepper. Mix vinegar, sugar and salt in a small bowl, whisk and pour over the cole slaw. Set aside in refrigerator.

Add 2 tbsp. vegetable oil to a pan, add onion and fry over low heat for 5 minutes. Add tomatoes and water or stock, let simmer over low heat for 30 minutes. Add jalapeño pepper, season to taste with salt and pepper. Set aside.

Sift flour in a bowl. Add water and knead into a smooth consistency.

Roll the dough into ten balls. Put a few drops of oil into the palm of your hand and shape one dough ball in your hand into a disk. Heap 1 tbsp. cheese mixture in the middle and fold again into a ball. Repeat with each ball.

Add 1 tbsp. vegetable oil to a heavy skillet. Cook the pupusa until golden brown, about 5 minutes. Turn and repeat with the other side.

Serve with tomato salsa and cole slaw.

INGREDIENTS

- 14 oz fresh queso blanco
  (or subsitute with mozzarella or other mild cheese)
- 1 cup loroco flour
- 1 lb corn flour
- 1 ¾ cups + 2 tbs warm water
- vegetable oil

Cole slaw
- ½ white cabbage, finely shredded
- 1 carrot, finely grated
- jalapeño pepper, cut into rings
- 4 tbsp. vinegar
- 1 tbsp. sugar
- 1 tsp. salt

Tomato salsa
- 2 tbsp. vegetable oil
- 1 onion, finely chopped
- 3 Roma tomatoes, finely chopped
- ⅓ cup +2 tbs water of chicken stock
- 1 jalapeño pepper, finely chopped
- pepper and salt

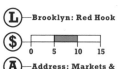

Ⓛ —Brooklyn: Red Hook

Ⓢ | 0 | 5 | 10 | 15

Ⓐ —Address: Markets & food courts F

Feasting in Red Hook

On a sunny Saturday or Sunday, I like to ride my bike over the Brooklyn Bridge and then through Brooklyn Bridge Park along the waterfront to Red Hook. Part of what lures me are the delicacies I can buy there, like the delectable **lobster rolls**, authentic **pupusa** and the tasty **key lime pie** Red Hook is famous for. I like to eat those al fresco, in a park or near the water. Out-of-the-way Red Hook is an old port district in Brooklyn that was the setting for the Marlon Brando movie *On the Waterfront*. In the 1990s, Red Hook had the reputation of being one of the most dangerous neighborhoods of America. Against all expectations, the area, like others in New York that seemed hopelessly decayed, made a comeback. There is a new Ikea megastore and a new Fairway supermarket which sells all kinds of delicacies. Artists have discovered the neighborhood. There are new galleries and restaurants on Van Brunt Street, the charming main street, and its side streets. There is also a sprawling complex of brick buildings, the Red Hook Projects, where the poorest live. During the warmer months, rich and poor go on the weekends to the Red Hook ball fields for the food trucks operated by chefs from Mexico, El Salvador, Colombia, the Dominican Republic and Guatemala.

The tradition of Latin American 'ball field vendors' began in 1974. The first vendors sold their wares on folding tables near the Red Hook ball fields. Everything was informal. Nobody had a license. The city authorities did not bother the vendors. They had more urgent problems at that time, such as fast rising crime, an epidemic of arson and urban flight. But a quarter century later, the tide had turned in Red Hook too. Meanwhile, word of mouth publicity had lured an increasing number of people from outside Red Hook to the Red Hook ball fields. Not to play sports but to savor the Latin American dishes. Media attention further fanned the food fest's popularity. Inevitably, the city's food inspectors came to take a look. The vendors appeared to be in violation of a variety of rules. Suddenly, the survival of the food fest was in jeopardy. Fortunately, the vendors could count on a great deal of sympathy from the public and the media. In 2008 – the year in which Ikea opened its megastore at a few minutes walking distance from the Red Hook ball fields – the city compromised with the vendors. From then on, only professional food trucks were allowed to sell food and they had to park at the edge of the park. For some vendors that was a mortal blow. A food truck costs at least 50.000 dollars, more than they could borrow. Others flourished. Although there are now fewer vendors than before, the weekly event remains a lively and very popular food fest. Some of the survivors, like the 'Country Boys/Martinez Taco Truck' have become so successful that they now have several trucks with which they also go to other street food events in Brooklyn. I prefer to visit the ball field vendors in the company of several people. That way, we can share the dishes. It's impossible to taste everything anyway. The choice is just too great. For 5 or 6 dollars, you can eat enough for the rest of the day. One piece of advice: take the time to sit quietly on the grass or a bench, to enjoy not just the food but also the colorful cocktail of people and languages. This is New York.

After tasting, I like to ride my bike along the waterfront of Red Hook, the old port installations, and the 19th century warehouses. Through smaller streets with old working class houses which are now insanely expensive, I ride to my next culinary destination. The Lobster Pound on Van Brunt Street is the pre-eminent place for fresh lobster rolls. The owners, Steve and Victoria Tarpin, travel every week to Maine to buy their lobsters. They keep the animals in big round tanks in their store. Tough, defrosted lobster meat is not served at this place.
One last culinary stop, this time for dessert. I ride to a huge, 19th century warehouse overlooking the bay of New York. There, at Steve's Authentic Key Lime Pie I buy my favorite dessert, made with the juice of the tiny limes of the Florida Keys. Lime pies are often too sweet. Steve's pie has just the right degree of acidity.

Then I bike to Ikea. I take the ferry between the store and the pier at Wall Street in Manhattan. The trip lasts 15 minutes. The views are breath taking. It doesn't have to be more than this for me on a summery Sunday in New York.

Until the 1870s lobster was cheap food in New York. The increasing water pollution made it an expensive delicacy. By the 1890s, lobster was associated with wealth and entertainment.

A popular image of that period was the dancing lobster with a top hat on and a pretty girl in his claw. That represented the wild spending bon vivant with his squeeze, the kind of people that were at home in the so-called Lobster Palaces.

Those luxurious, often enormous restaurants were concentrated in the area that is now Times Square. With the arrival of the gourmet food trucks and foodie markets like Smorgasburg, lobster has become street food again, albeit no longer at the democratic prices of yesteryear.

INGREDIENTS

- ½ cup celery, finely chopped
- 1 tbsp. lemon juice
- 4 tbsp. mayonnaise
- 2½ cups lobster meat, shredded
- salt and freshly ground black pepper to taste
- dash of paprika or Creole herbs or
  Cajun herb mixture
- 3 to 4 lightly toasted soft rolls
- 1 tbsp. butter or olive oil

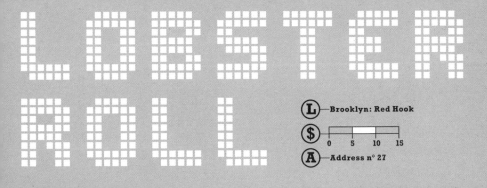

LOBSTER ROLL

(L)—Brooklyn: Red Hook

($) 0   5   10   15

(A)—Address n° 27

★ ★

The lobster sold in New York is usually caught in the cool waters along the Atlantic coast of North America. On the menu it's often called Maine lobster, after the state which is its most important supplier. The cold water lobster has more meat than its cousin the spiny rock lobster who lives in the warmer waters of Florida, the Caribbean and southern California.

STEP BY STEP!

\# In a bowl, mix the celery, lemon juice and mayonnaise. Add the lobster meat and season to taste with salt, pepper, paprika or Creole or Cajun herb mixture. Place in refrigerator.

\# Right before serving: cut open the rolls and brush the inside with melted butter or olive oil. Heat a grill pan over medium heat, place the roll buttered- face down on the grill for about 3 minutes. Repeat with the remaining rolls.

\# Heap the lobster meat on the grilled rolls and serve immediately.

Steve's authentic

KEY LIME PIE

★ ★ ★ ★

The key lime is a kind of lime named after the Key Islands in Florida, where it was grown until a hurricane destroyed most plantations. Nowadays, most key limes come from Mexico. They are smaller, rounder, more sour and bitter than the larger Persian lime. They are best when they're still unripe and green. Steve's authentic key lime pie is my favorite dessert. Steve Tarpin, who grew up in Florida, bakes his lime pies in an old warehouse in Red Hook. He supplies the best hotels and restaurants in New York. Connected to the bakery, there's a small store open to the public.

INGREDIENTS

For the crust
- 8 oz graham crackers, crushed
- 4 oz butter, melted

For the filling
- 1 cup canned sweetened condensed milk, chilled
- 4 egg yolks, cold
- ½ cup fresh key lime juice, cold
- whipped cream for garnish

* THERE'S MORE *

Not every key lime pie is the real thing. Some restaurants and bakeries use condensed lime juice which diminishes the quality.

STEP BY STEP!

PREPARE THE CRUST:

Preheat oven to 325 °F.

To make crust, combine the ingredients in a bowl and mix well for 2 minutes. Mold the mixture into a greased 10 inch pie shell and bake for 8 minutes or until golden brown.

Remove the crust from the oven and allow to cool.

PREPARE THE FILLING:

To make the filling, combine the milk and egg yolks and mix well. Slowly add the key lime juice and mix just until incorporated. Do not over mix or the pie will not set-up in the refrigerator.

Pour the mix into the pre-baked pie sheet and refrigerate until set.

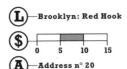

Ⓛ —Brooklyn: Red Hook

Ⓢ 0　5　10　15

Ⓐ —Address n° 20

New York needs its street vendors

'Can we trust this food?' European tourists ask me sometimes when they see the vast offer**ings** of food stands and food trucks in New York. My answer is: 'Absolutely.' Food stands are cleaner than many restaurants. The customer sees and smells the whole cooking event. When, for instance, the **fried bananas** or the **chicken with basil** are not fresh, the cook cannot camouflage this . Also good for the freshness is the fact that the food stands are rather small and don't have much space for storage. Not long ago I went to a stand in Chinatown, craving a favorite snack, a pancake with scallions that sells for one dollar. 'Sorry,' said the Chinese vendor who was packing his stuff, 'I'm all sold out. I'll be here again tomorrow.' It was 4 pm. The assumption that the preparation of food in the streets by immigrants from third world countries cannot be very hygienic is often made subconsciously, even by people who aren't racist at all. But experienced New Yorkers know better. Rich and poor buy food from street vendors. Empathy plays a role too. I have heard several Americans talk with pride about their grandfather or great-grandfather who came here without a penny in his pocket and speaking not a word of English, but started to work immediately as a street vendor. In the 19th and early 20th century, when there were still far fewer stores and restaurants, you could buy almost anything in the streets. With every new wave of immigration, the offer widened. The street food evolved too. Popular dishes over the centuries were oysters, pepper pot (stewed guts, bacon and vegetables), hard boiled eggs, grilled or cooked cobs of corn, gingerbread, crullers, roasted peanuts and chestnuts, baked pears in syrup, braised apples, apple cider, baked potatoes, coffee, sweet and hearty pastry, pretzels, pickles, knishes, hot dogs, bratwurst, Greek souvlaki and kebabs and, most recently, halal. The list is not complete. And we have to add as well the gourmet food trucks with their dazzling assortment of international dishes.

I tip my hat to the street vendors. It's hard work. You have to get up early. You're exposed to all kinds of weather. You have to stay friendly with your customers or they might not come back. Your working day is long. All sorts of people can make things difficult for you. The owners of the buildings in front of which you parked your stand, shopkeepers and even other street vendors who see you as competition. Worst of all is the police. The more vendors there are, the stricter it becomes. The increase of the number of gourmet food trucks in midtown Manhattan led in the summer of 2011 to an avalanche of parking tickets. Every day, about 700.000 people work in the offices, stores, hotels and theaters of midtown. Small wonder, then, that many street food vendors want to go to this area to peddle their wares. The large concentration of people creates a pressing shortage of parking space in the streets. And parking space is what those big gourmet food trucks need. They can't park on the sidewalk like a hot dog or halal cart can. And since 2011 they are no longer allowed to park at parking meters. This rule was disastrous for the food trucks since there are parking meters everywhere in the busiest part of midtown. By the end of 2012 the police became a bit more flexible, but for most food trucks, it remains a daily cat and mouse game.

→ continues on p. 099

Because plantains are eaten
in many different tropical
regions, there are many
recipes to prepare them.
It's a perfect fruit for cooks
to e experiment with.
They can be steamed, cooked,
fried, grilled or deep-fried.

(L)—**Manhattan: Harlem**

($)—

| 0 | 5 | 10 | 15 |

(A)—**Address n° 04**

INGREDIENTS

- 2 ripe plantains (skin may be yellow or black)
- 4 tbsp. olive oil or butter

FRIED
PLANTAINS

The tropical plantains are green, hard bananas, very rich in starch. Unlike the sweet yellow bananas, they are never eaten raw. They are cooked or fried. The taste resembles that of potatoes somewhat. When they are overripe, they taste a bit sweeter. Since millions of New Yorkers come from places where plantains are a daily staple, they are a common sight in supermarkets.

STEP BY STEP!

Peel and cut the plantains in pieces about ½ inch thick

In a non-stick skillet, heat the oil or butter. Over medium low heat, fry the plantains in a single layer until golden on the bottom then turn over with a spatula. Cook for a few more minutes.

Drain excess oil on paper towels. Serve after 2 to 3 minutes.

> Hot and spicy, like at a Thai market… Khrapao basil gives this dish an irresistible aroma.

KHAO PAT KHRAPAO GAI

(L) — Manhattan: Midtown

($) 0 5 10 15

>>

STIR-FRIED CHICKEN WITH THAI BASIL

INGREDIENTS

- 2 tbsp. vegetable oil
- 2 cloves garlic, mashed
- 1 Thai chili pepper (optional)
- 5 oz chicken fillet, minced
- 1 or 2 Chinese long beans,
  cut into ⅓ inch rings
  (about 2 tbsps.)
- 1 tbsp. light soy sauce
- 1 tbsp. fish sauce
- ¼ tbsp. sugar
- 3 tbsps. chicken broth
- 30 khrapao basil leaves

Garnish (optional)
- cucumber slices
- egg sunny side up
- phrik nam pla (5 tbsps. fish sauce,
  3 tbsps. lime juice, 4 bird's eye
  chilies or Thai chili peppers)

STEP BY STEP!

Heat a wok over low heat, add the oil immediately. Add the garlic and stir-fry for 30 seconds. Add the chili pepper and stir-fry for another 30 seconds.

Over medium heat, add the minced chicken. Stir-fry till the meat is browned. Add the long beans. Add some water or chicken broth if necessary.

Add the soy sauce, fish sauce and sugar. Stir-fry for 1 minute and add some water or chicken stock. Very briefly stir-fry the basil leaves and scoop the now ready mixture out of the wok.

Serve on a bed of rice with cucumber slices, a fried egg sunny side up and phrik nam pla.

Variations with pork or beef or
mushrooms vegetarian-style
work equally well.

✦ ✦ ✦ ✦ ✦ ✦ ✦ ✦ ✦ ✦ ✦ ✦ ✦ ✦ ✦ ✦ ✦ ✦

Repression → continuation of p. 092

Like the yellow cabs and the oldest skyscrapers, the food stands are signature New York. In other American cities, they're a much rarer sight. And yet, the city government doesn't make life easy for the street vendors. The first law on food stands dates back to the end of the 19th century. Vendors could stay **at** the same place no longer than half an hour and then had to move on. It was hard to enforce this law, especially in overpopulated neighborhoods like the Lower East Side. In 1886 street vendors founded a push cart market on Hester Street. It was lively but also chaotic. There were complaints about corruption and unsanitary conditions. In 1928 the city decided that street vendors had to be licensed and it limited the number of licenses to 7000. But in the 1930s, when the Great Depression caused massive unemployment, many saw no other way to survive then to become street vendors. Some had only a few apples to peddle. Most were unlicensed. Mayor LaGuardia wanted to radically repress the street vending. He prohibited the sale of food on most streets and forced the vendors to rent a space in a covered market. One of those markets, the Essex Street Market on the Lower East Side, still exists. The other covered markets did not survive. New Yorkers have always preferred open air markets. LaGuardia's prohibition of street vending was very unpopular and had to be withdrawn.

But having a license remained obligatory for street vendors. And the number of licenses remained limited. It was even lowered sharply in 1988 by Mayor Koch, even though he liked to boast that his father had been a street vendor too. Only 3000 food vendors (and 853 other street vendors) received a license. In practice, many more remained active. But now they risked fines and confiscation. The next mayor who tried to chase the street vendors away, was Giuliani. In 1998 he made their presence illegal on 144 street blocks in downtown and midtown Manhattan. But just like LaGuardia he encountered strong headwinds and had to back down. After all, the streets of fast-moving, bustling New York are unimaginable without the street vendors. The role they play, economically, socially and in culinary terms, is just too important.

Still, the city keeps making their lives difficult. Under Mayor Bloomberg the fines on illegal street vending were ratcheted up. At the same time, the shortage of licences leaves most vendors no other option but to work illegally. In 2012 there were 4000 licenses for street vendors of food and 1700 for vendors of other wares. The number of street vendors that year was estimated to be 25.000. So more than 19.000 of them work unlicensed and have to accept the occasional fines and confiscations of their merchandise as part of their normal operating costs. Meanwhile, more and more licenses are getting into ever fewer hands. Eight companies, who together own a third of the licenses, have founded the Big Apple Food Association. They rent out licensed food carts and sit back, watching the money flow in. Meanwhile, the street vendors struggle to keep their heads above water.

→ continues on p. 186

→ continuation of p. 063

Enough biking for one day. In the evening I leave the bike home and join my friend Gabby, who lives in New York, on the Lower East Side, for beers. A bit later we sit on a terrace and feast on an authentic Puerto Rican meal. It's as if we're sitting at the table of our Puerto Rican grandma who wants to stuff us till we burst. Rarely have I been received so warmly in a restaurant. We can't buy beer here but that's no problem; we buy it in the store next door. And no need to chose among dishes, since cook Nelly knows what's good for us: mofongo (flattened bananas with pork meat), pernil (grilled pork shoulder) and chicharrones (fried chicken). These simple dishes from Puerto Rico's basic cuisine are prepared with love and warmth. That we can taste.

The next day I call Jeff Ollick and tell him I'd like to dig deeper into the local street food scene. Jeff has a fulltime job but on top of it he gives (street) food tours of Jackson Heights in Queens. So I'm glad that he has some time for me. Before I am to meet him on 111th Street in Jackson Heights, I take the number 7 subway train all the way to the last station, Flushing. My hope is to find some inspiration here for my future noodle bar. Flushing is a lively neighborhood and New York's second Chinatown. I feel like a fish in the water; there is a gregarious bustle comparable with the vibe of a big Asian city. Nowadays, New York has three Chinese neighborhoods or 'Asiatowns': in lower Manhattan, in Brooklyn's Sunset Park and here in Flushing Queens. I wander through a super market and imagine myself in Taipei, Saigon or Bangkok. Water spinach, long Chinese beans, Thai basil… the delicious stench of durian. Asians with push carts, clearing their way through the crowd. A staircase going up and an escalator going down lead me to an underground food court. It's easy to see the resemblance to a Singapore Hawker Centre. In the center, there are enough seats to eat more or less quietly. I inspect the imaginatively made billboards and colorful pictures and eventually choose the **Szechuan chicken**. Szechuan is one of the most hearty Chinese cuisines and I can stand a good portion of Szechuan pepper, which has a delicious aroma. Back on the street, New York treats me to one of its typical autumnal showers. I run around the corner and find shelter under the railway bridge on Main Street. Under an antique sign board, behind tiny fogged windows, three ladies are making **pancakes with scallions**. They smell wonderful and cost only 75 cents apiece. Accross the street, a Chinese man is grilling skewered meats over charcoal. His sign says: ''Xinjiang Barbecue'. The rain keeps pouring down. I ask the few locals who venture outside where I can find wonton soup but nobody seems to understand me. Finally, a young student whose mastery of English is better, directs me to a food court a bit further **down** on Main Street. I pass it three times before I find it, hidden behind in a tiny stairwell. I'm drenched when I go down the yellow steps which bring me into another world. The modest food court serves, among other delicacies, **Xian noodles**, delectably smelling noodles with lamb meat in a hearty sauce with a slight hint of cumin. I also find **wonton soup**, a typical dish from Hong Kong. A bit further I see **Chinese rolls filled with pork meat**. Again those delicious rolls, I saw them earlier in Momofuku. I look forward to making them myself when I'm back home.

My encounter with Jeff Ollick is one of the high points of my stay in New York. Jeff has a sober mind and a passion for street food, and for the people who put their hearts and souls into it every day. We meet at the Tortas Neza food truck, where he orders, for the two of us, **taco with salted beef and green chili sauce**. A taco, a small filled tortilla, is one of the most popular street food dishes in New York. What a joy for my taste buds, a chili sauce, I never tasted before. I lick it from my fingers and grin broadly from sheer happiness. And I haven't even tasted the tortas! The different tortas, which look like mutated cheeseburgers on steroïds, are named after Mexican soccer teams. Owner Galdino Molinaro proposes to make a super torta. The monster that is heading our way is spread with cabbage, tomatoes, avocado, chipotle sauce, homemade bean paste, three deep-fried frankfurters, four slices of ham, a few slices of Mexican cheese and crumbled chicken fillet. He presses the sandwich closed, grills it on a hot plate and turns it over a couple of times. Then he wraps it in aluminum foil and cuts it in half. And there you have it: sandwichzilla! I can hardly believe this is supposed to be for just one person. Eating it without spilling is impossible.

→ continues on p. 118

北京片皮鴨

腸粉 / 北京鴨
RICE WRAP / PEKING DUCK

蝦仁腸粉
Shrimp Rice Roll
$2.50

早上七時
至下午三時
7AM - 3PM
腸粉
即叫即蒸
Make to Order Steam Rice Roll
另加雞蛋 Add Egg $0.50/粒

叉燒腸粉
Roast Pork Rice Roll
$1.50

豬肉腸粉
Pork Rice Roll
$1.50

牛肉腸粉

蝦米腸粉
$1.50

.799

Honey Kist

HAMI
GOLD

新鮮
$4.99

$1.00/片 Pc.
鴨殼 Duck Bone
$2.50/隻 Ea.

北京片

Marinate the chicken in 1 tbsp. soy sauce, the rice wine and the sesame oil for 30 minutes.

Heat a wok over medium heat, add 2 tbsp. vegetable oil and fry the shallot, garlic and celery for about 1 minute. Add the jalapeño pepper.

Remove the chicken from the marinade. Set aside the marinade. Add the chicken to the wok and stir fry until the strips are browned all over. Add 1 tbsp. water and 1 tbsp. soy sauce. Add the marinade and sugar.

Add the chives and szechuan pepper and stir fry for 30 seconds.

INGREDIENTS

- 2 chicken fillets, cut into strips
- 2 tbsp. light soy sauce
- 2 tbsp. Shaoxing rice wine
- 2 tsp. sesame oil
- 2 shallots, coarsely chopped
- 2 cloves garlic, mashed
- 1 celery stalk, coarsely chopped
- 2 tbsp. vegetable oil
- 4 jalapeño chili peppers, coarsely chopped
- 1 tbsp. water
- ½ tbsp. sugar
- 2 chives, coarsely chopped
- 1 tsp. szechuan pepper, roasted and finely ground
- steamed rice

This will delight your taste buds!

SZECHUAN
STIR-FRIED
CHICKEN

THERE'S MORE

Szechuan pepper is not a chili pepper but a pepper berry. It is related to the citrus family; the taste is sharp rather than pungent. The Szechuan kitchen is considered to be the most hearty of the five main Chinese cuisines.

INGREDIENTS

- 2 cups flour
- 2 tsp. salt
- 1 tsp. sugar
- 1 tsp. dry yeast dissolved in ½ cup lukewarm water
- 3 tbsp. vegetable oil
- 5 scallions, finely chopped

Scallion pancake

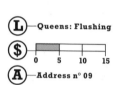

L — Queens: Flushing

$ 0 5 10 15

A — Address n° 09

★ ★

Under a bridge in Jackson Heights I discovered this nutritious cheap snack.

STEP BY STEP!

In a bowl, sift the flower and add the salt. Add the sugar to the yeast and water. Pour the water on the flour and knead. Add 2 tbsp. vegetable oil. Cover the dough with a clean kitchen towel and let rest for 45 minutes at room temperature.

Sprinkle some flour on clean work surface. Divide the dough into clumps the size of golf balls. Use a rolling pin to flatten to about 6 inch circles.

Scatter the chopped scallions on top. Roll up the dough, making sure the scallions remain in place. Place upright and roll again with the rolling pin to flatten to about 6 inch circles.

In a skillet heat 2 tbsp. vegetable oil over medium heat. Cook the pancake on both sides for about 5 minutes total till golden brown.

Sprinkle a few roasted sesame seeds,
fennel seeds or cumin on the dough
for an extra culinary note.

* *

STEP BY STEP!

\# In a skillet add 2 tbsp. vegetable oil and fry the onion till soft. Add the cumin, garlic, chili and meat. Stir- fry for 2 minutes. Add soy sauce and pepper. Stir- fry for another minute or till the meat is browned on all sides.

\# Add ⅓ cup water. Let simmer on low heat for 30 minutes. Add salt.

\# Meanwhile cook the noodles. Rinse under cold water to prevent sticking. Drain and add the noodles to the lamb meat. Stir.

\# Stir in the chives and serve.

INGREDIENTS

- 2 tbsp. vegetable oil
- 1 onion, julienned
- 1 tbsp. cumin seeds, roasted
- 2 cloves garlic, mashed
- 1 tsp. chili powder
- 1 lb lamb shoulder, cut into 1 inch
  by 1 inch chunks
- 2 tbsp. soy sauce
- ½ tsp. black pepper
- ⅓ cup water
- pinch of salt
- 10 oz broad yellow rice noodles,
  cooked according to package
- cooking water from the noodles
- 4 chives, cut diagonally in 1 inch
  pieces

SPICY LAMB NOODLES

(L)—Queens: Flushing

($)— 0 5 10 15

(A)—Address n° 14

Thick, flat, handmade or dried noodles go together well with this preparation of pungently spiced lamb meat.

- 7 oz chopped pork
- 1 ⅓ oz shrimp, finely chopped
- 1 tbsp. light soy sauce
- 2 chives, finely chopped
- ¼ tsp. white pepper
- 1 tsp. ginger, minced
- 4 cups clear chicken broth
- 20 wonton skins
- 1 chive, cut into rings
- 2 leaves Napa cabbage, coarsely chopped

* THERE'S MORE *

Wontons can also be deep-fried. Then they are great in soups or as an appetizer with a sweet and sour dipping sauce.

WONTON SOUP

with pork, scampi & ginger

I tasted this soup for the first time in Hong Kong, wonton country!

Ⓛ—**Queens: Flushing**

$ | 0 | 5 | 10 | 15

STEP BY STEP!

Start with preparing the wonton filling. Mix the meat with the shrimp, light soy sauce, chives, pepper and ginger. Set aside.

Bring the chicken broth to a boil.

Take a wonton skin, heap 1 tsp. of the filling in the middle. Close the skin into a triangle. Bring the left and right corner of the wonton together above the filling and press. Moisten your fingers with some water to seal the wonton. Repeat with the remaining wonton skins.

Add the cabbage to the chicken broth, add the wonton. Cook for 5 minutes.

Serve in soup bowls and garnish with chive rings.

金商場

HOPPING MALL

小吃一條街

FOOD COURT

DOWN STAIR

BRAND NAME FOR LESS	
BRAND NAME FOR LESS	
名牌服裝折扣店	
33 榮豐堂保健品	
27 夢想時裝屋	
28 花店	
2 閩東影視	
de Noodle 蘭州拉面	

1A 南北水餃	31 成都天府小吃
15	15 四季面
16 溫州朱记小吃	26 西安名吃
32 溫州小吃	29 全家富沙縣小吃

I'm Garlic
Marinated Ch
nd I'm Super S

INGREDIENTS

Pulled pork
- 2 pounds pork shoulder

For the marinade
- 3 ½ oz (approximately 5 tbsp.) salt
- 3 ½ oz (approximately 8 tbsp.) sugar
- ¾ cup + 2 tbsp. water
- 2 bay leaves
- 2 tbsp. of the following herb blend:

Dry herb blend
- 1 tbsp. cumin powder
- 1 tbsp. chili powder
- 1 tbsp. paprika
- 1 tbsp. garlic powder
- 1 tsp. salt
- 1 tsp. black pepper
- 2 tbsp. sugar
- vegetable oil

For the bun
- 1. ½ cups water
- 1 tsp. dry yeast
- 6 tbsp. sugar
- 2 lbs all-purpose flour
- 1 tbsp. salt
- ½ tsp. baking powder
- ½ tsp. baking soda
- vegetable oil

Serve with
- hoisin sauce
- Sriracha chili sauce

Gwa pao or steamed buns are still a popular street food in Taipei.

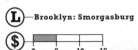

Brooklyn: Smorgasburg

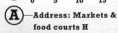

0 5 10 15

Address: Markets & food courts H

PULLED PORK BUN
♥ ♥ ♥ or *Steamed* buns ♥ ♥ ♥
originated in *Taiwan*

STEP BY STEP!

\# Rinse the pork shoulder under cold water. Pat dry. Put the meat in a plastic bag.

\# In a mixing bowl, add all the ingredients for the marinade and blend well. Add to the pork shoulder, close the bag tightly and let marinate for 6 hours.

\# In a mixing bowl, add the water, yeast and sugar, blend well. Add the water to the flour, add salt, baking powder, baking soda and 2 tbsp. oil. Knead for 30 minutes by hand or 15 minutes in a kneading machine.

\# Cover with a dry cloth. Let rise for 1 hour or till the quantity has doubled.

\# Sprinkle some flour on a work surface. Use a rolling pin to roll the dough into a disk. Roll up and work into a long cylinder. Cut the dough into small golf ball size pieces. Arrange the pieces in one layer on a platter, cover with a dry cloth and let rise again for approximately 1 hour.

\# Again sprinkle some flour on a work face. Roll each dough ball into an oval of about 3 inches by 5 ½ inches. Dip a chop stick into oil. Put the chop stick in the middle of the oval. Fold one half of dough over the other. Close the top. Repeat with the rest of the dough. Arrange the buns again on the platter, cover with cloth and let rise for another 30 minutes.

\# Remove the pork meat from the marinade. Pat dry. Rub the meat with the dry herb blend.

\# Heat the oven to 400 °F . Arrange the meat on an oven rack and roast for 45 minutes. Turn down to 225 °F and let roast for another 90 minutes.

\# Remove meat from oven. Let cool a bit. Pull the meat apart with a fork.

\# Steam 4 to 5 buns at a time for about 15 minutes till done. Remaining unused buns can be frozen.

\# Add 1 tbsp. hoisin sauce to the inside of the steamed bun. Add some pulled pork. Serve with Sriracha chili sauce.

SALTED BEEF TACO

★ ★

WITH LEMON & CHILI

INGREDIENTS

- 8 cups water
- 4 tbsp. salt
- 3 tbsp. sugar
- ½ tsp. black pepper, coarsely ground
- 1 lb beef
- 1 tbsp. chili powder
- ½ tsp. black pepper
- ½ tsp. cumin
- 10-15 tacos

Green chili sauce
- 1 onion, finely chopped
- 2 cloves garlic, finely chopped
- 2 tbsp. vegetable oil
- 1 pound green tomato, peeled
- water
- ½ tsp. dried oregano
- 3 green serrano chili peppers, roasted, finely chopped
- 1 tsp. salt

Garnish
- lime slices
- green chili sauce
- handful fresh cilantro, chopped

STEP BY STEP!

\# In a pot, add 4 cups water, add the salt, sugar and pepper. Bring to a boil, turn off the heat and let cool.

\# Pierce the meat with a fork on all sides. Add the meat to the water and let it sit for a minimum of 24 hours. Put a weight on top of the meat so that it stays submerged. Remove the meat, rinse well.

\# Meanwhile prepare the green chili sauce. In a skillet add 1 tbsp. oil, fry the onion and garlic till soft. Add the tomatoes and cook briefly. Cover with water. Add the oregano and let simmer over low heat for about an hour or till the water is evaporated.

\# Put the tomatoes and chili peppers in a blender and mix well. Add 1 tbsp. vegetable oil in a pot and heat up the tomato mixture for 5 minutes. Add salt. Let cool.

\# Heat 4 cups of water in a pot. Add chili powder, black pepper and cumin. Bring to a boil and let the meat simmer over low heat for 90 minutes. Let the meat cool and cut into thin strips.

\# Fry the tacos according to the package's instructions.

\# Add 1 to 2 tbsp. of the meat to the taco and serve with lime slices, green chili sauce and fresh cilantro.

Salted beef is a delicious snack on tacos. Add lime for a real taste sensation!

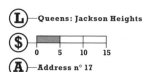

(L)—Queens: Jackson Heights

($) 0 5 10 15

(A)—Address n° 17

→ continuation of p. 101

We each wolf down half a torta and I have to admit it's a delightful taste bomb. Jeff's blood pressure and heart beat seem under control. He tells me the tortas are selected for the Vendy Awards. Because Galdino has no driver's license, Jeff drove the truck to the festival site. It shows his passion and unselfishness. Later, I will encounter such helpfulness again and again in the streets of New York.

We walk in Jackson Heights under the elevated tracks of the number 7 train, make a few right turns and enter the tortilla shop Nixtamal. In this colorful little house, tortilla are made artisanally. They even make their own flour. Co-owner Fernando Ruiz, who's wearing an 'I love Nixtamal'-T-shirt, shows us the machines used every morning to make fresh flour. We order some beers with appropriate snacks. An item on the menu peaks my curiosity: **cactus salad**, I never tasted that before. The taste of the cactus is not very pronounced but the cotija cheese lifts it to a higher level. We continue our trip through Jackson Heights. On 86th Street we look for the world famous **tamale** lady, but unfortunately she's not there at this time. There are no guarantees regarding opening hours and locations. Better luck next time. Further down the street we meet a man on a bike who's selling tacos from under a blue plastic tarp. A bit further still, an elderly woman sells **elotes** under a Sabrett umbrella. Young kids gather around her cart, order elotes and divide them among themselves. Workers on their way home stop for a quick bite at the Dominican food carts. The whole street suddenly comes alive. Jeff and I finish our walk **on** 74th Street, the largest Indian neighborhood in New York. Over a distance of just a few kilometers, we have traveled from China through Mexico and the Dominican Republic.

→ continues on p. 128

INGREDIENTS

- 1 can nopales or 1 medium sized fresh
  cactus pad (leaf), cut into 1 inch pieces and
  simmered to the desired softness
- 2 fresh tomatoes, cubed
- 1 green pepper, cubed
- 1 onion, sliced
- a few radishes
- 1 chili pepper, jalapeño
- ½ tsp. salt
- juice of ½ lime
- 1 tbsp. olive oil
- 3 tbsp. cotija cheese, crumbled
- 1 handful fresh cilantro leaves

CACTUS SALAD *Fresh and tasty*

* **THERE'S MORE** *

If you use fresh nopales, be careful, because they get slimy when they're cooked too long. Spanish conquerors brought this cactus from Mexico to Europe. From there, it also spread to North Africa.

Ⓛ —Queens: Jackson Heights

$

0   5   10   15

Ⓐ —Address n° 26

> What a discovery. I didn't even know that you could eat them!

STEP BY STEP!

\# Toss the cactus with the tomato, green pepper, radish, onion and chili pepper in a salad bowl. Add salt to taste, lime juice and olive oil. Toss again.

\# Add the cotija cheese on top and garnish with the fresh cilantro.

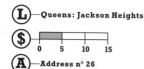

L — Queens: Jackson Heights

$ 0 5 10 15

A — Address n° 26

This way of cooking and then pulling apart pork meat, is the basic technique for pulled pork, which features in many American dishes. It's fun to experiment with the filling: vegetarians may try this with finely chopped seasoned fried mushrooms.

TAMALE

★ ★

Steamed pork in corn husks

STEP BY STEP!

Trim fat from the pork shoulder.
Put the meat, onion and garlic in a pot. Add water and bring to a boil. Cover.
Let simmer for 2 hours over low heat.

Remove the meat and let cool. Shred the meat in a bowl, add salt and chili powder, stir and set aside.

In a bowl, sift the masa flour, add salt and baking powder. Add lard and butter, blend well. Add chicken stock, using wire whisk to mix.

Take 1 corn husk, deposit 2 tbsp. masa-mixture in the middle. Spread evenly over the leaf, leaving ½ inch uncovered on each side.

Deposit 1 tbsp. of the pork on the dough but keep the edges of the dough free.

Roll up midway, fold in the edges and roll up further. Close by tying a small piece of kitchen twine around the tamale.

Steam for an hour till the husk easily separates from the dough.

INGREDIENTS

- 1¼ pound pork shoulder
- 8 cups water
- 1 onion, cut in half
- 2 cloves garlic, mashed
- 1 tsp. salt
- ½ tsp. chili powder
- 1¼ cup masa flour
- 1 tsp. salt
- 1 tsp. baking powder
- 2 tsp. lard
- 2 tsp. butter
- ⅓ cup + 2 tbsp. chicken stock
- 10 dried corn husks (hojas), soaked in water for 15 minutes

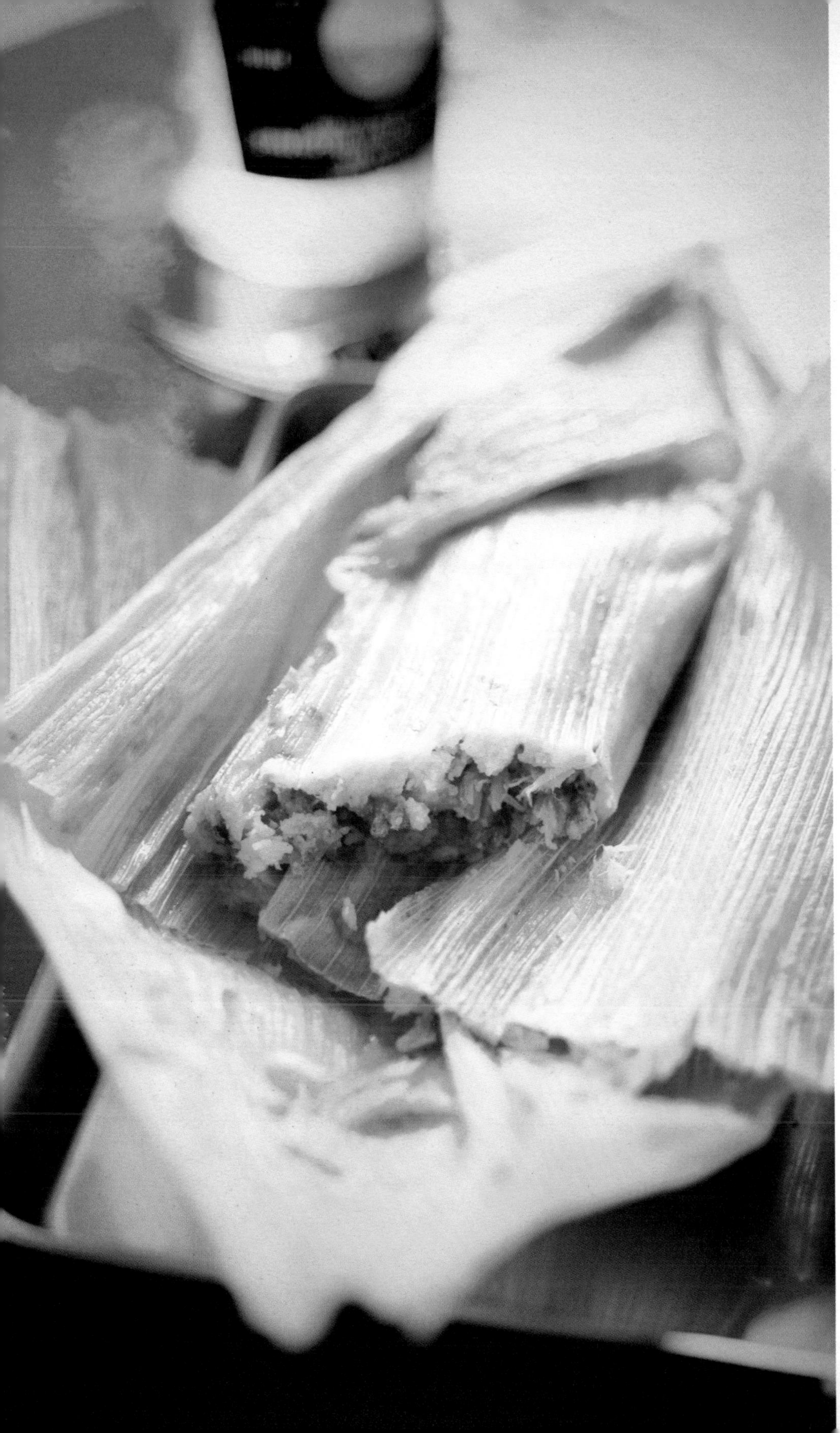

'The best tamales of New York'

Our Lady of Guadalupe is the patron saint of Mexico. In New York she has her own church on 14th street in Chelsea. Every Sunday there are five masses, three in Spanish and two in English. The church is filled every time. That's the reason why Marina Vera Luz has been here every Sunday morning for twenty years, operating a very popular food stand. On the sidewalk in front of the church she treats the hungry parishioners with a wide offer of Mexican soups, tamales and tortas in grandma-style. 'I have other customers too,' she tells us in Spanish, 'cops and firemen, people who work in hotels and restaurants in the neighborhood and tourists from Spain and Latin America.' Don't let Marina's sweet modest smile fool you. This is a tough woman. She lives with her family in East Harlem.

'Every night, I get up at 2 am,' she tells me. 'During the week I sell tamales from 5 to 8 am at the corner of 40th Street and 8th Avenue. On Saturdays, I sleep a little longer. On Saturday afternoons, I shop for all that you see here. In the evening a lady friend arrives and we cook together throughout the night. By morning, my husband and my son load everything into our van. We arrive here by 6 am. People already start lining up while we're still unpacking.

We work until we're sold out. Usually, that's around 3 or 4 pm. By then, I'm exhausted. When I get home, I go to bed immediately, because I have to get up the next day at 2 am again.' I ask her if she sometimes skips a Sunday. 'Never,' she says proudly. 'Rain or snow, she can't be stopped,' says her husband Moises. With a twinkle in his eyes he adds: 'And I always have to go with her.'

The couple is from Mexico City. 'We came to New York in 1987,' Moises recounts. Another man is listening in. His name is Riony and he's from Bolivia. 'Marina makes the best tamales of New York', he says enthusiastically. 'I've known her for ten years. I used to work not far from the place where she is on weekdays. At the job, we had a rotation schedule for standing in line. Every day, one of us bought tamales for everybody. It sometimes happened that one went too late and everything was sold out. Boy oh boy, did he get it! Now, I live and work in New Jersey. Every Sunday, I visit family in East Harlem, but first I stop here to buy tamales. I don't think they would let me in if I didn't bring them!'

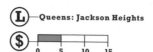

Ⓛ —Queens: Jackson Heights

$ 0 5 10 15

ELOTES

The typical Mexican street food!

STEAMED (OR GRILLED) CORN

INGREDIENTS

- 4 husked corn cobs
- 3 tbsp. mayonnaise
- juice of ½ lime
- 4 tbsp. cotija or parmesan cheese, grated
- ½ tsp. chili powder
- ½ tsp. salt
- ¼ tsp. cumin powder

* THERE'S MORE *

A variation of elotes is called esquites. For this, the corn cobs first are boiled, then shucked. Serve the kernels in a cup, in a dressing or mayonnaise (and/or sour cream), lime, cheese and chili.

STEP BY STEP!

Place the corn in a steambasket with some water. Steam for 15 minutes.

In a narrow and deep pot, mix the mayonnaise with the lime juice. Set aside.

In a bowl, mix the cheese, chili powder, salt and cumin.

Put a satay stick through the length of each corn cob. Roll the corn in the mayo mix and sprinkle cheese all over.

Serve warm.

A WALK ON THE WILD SIDE...

A few months later and after a lot of desk research I return to New York, this time with my friend photographer Luk Thys. We have only one goal: to roam the streets and neighborhoods with Jacqueline in search of the visible and hidden street food pearls of New York. The first days we stay in Red Hook and we scout the neighborhood with gusto. We eat sandwiches at Defontes and treat ourselves to **lobster rolls**.

We take the number 5 train from Brooklyn and get out at Union Square, where there is a greenmarket. The concept of the greenmarkets, local producers who supply healthy foods to city dwellers, originated about 30 years ago. Today, there are more than 70 greenmarkets in New York. The one in Union Square is bursting with organic tomatoes, fresh cobs of corn, many kinds of cabbages. It's a mistake to think that in the US everybody is hooked on pizza, milk shakes and cheeseburgers. The greenmarkets prove that there is a huge demand for fresh quality products. About ten food trucks are parked near Union Square. By now, I recognize some. Among the trucks I see Rafael Samanez with his Peruvian food stall Morocho. The Peruvian cuisine is considered one of the finest of South America. So I let myself be seduced. My sense of adventure makes me order the **veal heart saté with black mint sauce**. It's a caress for the tongue. Rafael tells us about his project Vamos Unidos, which aims to unite the street vendors. But we don't have much time, as Jacqueline is waiting for us. After a hearty goodbye, we're on our way.

Already from a distance we see Jacqueline in front of the Italian delicatessen Eataly, near the Flatiron building. She is sitting, with a cup of hot chocolate, on one of the chairs provided by the city of New York. 'Public seating,' or so this great initiative is called. We walk together through Eataly. Never have I seen such an extensive food concept. In Eataly you can find everything that's tasty and Italian. Fresh pastas in all imaginable forms, ripened pecorino with pepper from southern Italy, provolone, mouth-watering panna cotta and an excellent selection of wines. But the 'vegetable butcher' who cuts your vegetables for you, is, for me, as a cook, one step too far. While I still try to wrap my mind around this overwhelming offering, Jacqueline proposes a trip to the Bronx.

We take the B-train, hop off at the Grand Concourse in the South Bronx and walk to Fordham Road. Around the corner on Webster Road we see a small Dominican food stand. They sell alcapurrias, fritters made of mashed green plantains, yautia and other starchy tropical tubers, with heavily seasoned meat at the center, and tostones, salted slices of plantains twice fried with salami. They have also **papa rellena**, fritters with a filling of potato and beef. I order two of them. The filling is nicely smooth and the sour chili sauce makes the snack perfect. My drink has the inspiring name '**morir soñando**', which means 'to die dreaming.' The owner makes this heavenly brew herself, without kitchen appliances, with a base of condensed milk and orange juice. She shakes it until it has the right consistency and then pours it elegantly into a glass of crushed ice. As the name suggests, it's a devilish heavenly drink. The dean of the nearby university also stands in line. While he orders his satay, he assures us this is the best Dominican food stall in the neighborhood. Another favorite of his is Lucia's stand, which sells delicious Mexican **quesadillas**. We don't need more encouragement than that. Across a small junk market, Lucia is standing in a big kiosk. She tells us she has many customers who come eat oatmeal in the morning. She proposes that we try her **burritos and pork meat in a green sauce**. They confirm her reputation. Luckily, we still have a tiny spot left in our stomachs for these blissful warm snacks.

We walk a bit slower down the boulevard and make a left on Arthur Avenue. We pass a couple of typical Italian restaurants and the oyster bar Coseza's. We enter an indoor market specializing in Italian products. Near the entrance, there's a man hand rolling cigars. The ceiling is decorated with Italian and American flags. Women walk by with well-filled shopping bags. Suddenly, we're in an authentic Italian market place. The smells and atmosphere remind me of Sicily. The man in the meat department sits like a king between the salame abruzzese, proscuito di Parma and mortadella. He reminds me of Tony of the 'Sopranos.' We sit down at a table with a red-white striped tablecloth and order an espresso at the coffee bar. The guy behind the counter just bought a new espresso machine and still needs some practice. Relieved when he finally succeeds, he brings us the steaming coffee in pretty cups. We have the honor to taste the first coffee from his new machine.

After our coffee break we jump in a taxi to look for African street food. I had read that there is a big African market in the Bronx around this time. Jacqueline proposes to take a look around 167th Street. We ask around but we can't find the market. A clever Ghanaian spots an opportunity and brings us to a restaurant owned by a member of his family. On the menu we see pictures of several stews named 'fufu.' I never heard about it but it looks delicious and I wonder how it tastes. But after our culinary adventures of that day, it would be too much. Despite our fascination with the dish we decide to come back later, when our appetite can do honor to the fufu.

→ continues on p. 170

THIS WAY
EAT LOCAL

BROOKLYN BEAN COMPANY

AVAILABLE FROZEN $16/qurt CHILI $8/cup
MANGALITSA PORK FROM MOSEFUND FARM
LOCAL OR
VEGETARIAN
BOTH W/ THE WORKS

Greenmarkets

When I travel, I like to visit markets. There's no better place to learn something quickly about the local population. Stalls loaded with vegetables, fruits, flowers, bread, pastry, cheese, meat and fish in a small town in the Ardennes, a village in the Landes or a bustling neighborhood in Bangkok: if I can, I rummage around. In New York too, I go to the market regularly. I recommend it to all my visitors from abroad. The greenmarket on Union Square, where I'm walking around on this beautiful Saturday in October, is my favorite market. It's pretty busy today but nobody seems impatient. The greenmarket has an undeniable soothing effect. To shop here means to sniff the countryside and take a bit of it home. The entire colorful gamma of New Yorkers strolls by: people who look like they stepped out of fashion magazines, men in expensive tailored suits, black nannies with white babies, Indian women in saris, workers in splattered coveralls. The stands are a feast for the eye. I count more than twenty kinds of potatoes, with names like Russian Banana, Rozetta Indian and Butterball. At the stand of a red-cheeked girl I buy sorrel, a rare delicacy in New York. She also sells about twenty kinds of other fresh greens with exotic names like mizuna and tatsoi. A boy with long blond hair hands me a glass of fresh pear cider. Behind him there are shelves stuffed with yellow, rust-colored, purple and white chrysanthemums, surrounded by mountains of apples, pears and tomatoes. An Asian man has arranged his dizzying offer of peppers, with names like Hot Portugal and Inferno, artfully in little boxes. 'The last fresh sweet corn of the year,' a sign next to a big pile of corn announces. The squashes, stars of the American fall, steal the show. They have names like Stripetti, Butternut, Carnival and Delicata. At the fish stand it's really busy. 'We catch our fish ourselves with our boat, the Blue Moon,' a sign says. In the stand next to it, a man offers me a morsel of cheese. It tastes delicious. 'I made it myself', he says, 'it's inspired by the cheese of the Trappist monks.'

New York has 70 greenmarkets like this one. Not just anybody can peddle his wares there. Everything you sell, you have to have raised, grown or made yourself. Pesticides, antibiotics and genetically manipulated ingredients are strictly taboo. Independent inspectors control stringently. Many New Yorkers are willing to pay a little more for the merchandise at a greenmarket. It's not an elitist concept. In poorer neighborhoods such as the South Bronx too, greenmarket farmers spoil their customers with fresh delicacies every week. All vendors, even in the richer neighborhoods, accept food stamps.

The greenmarket began as a modest little market in Manhattan in 1976. Today, the 70 markets are co-ordinatated by an efficiently managed non-profit. On a Saturday in the high season there are 140 stands at Union Square Market which are visited, on average, by 60,000 people. That makes the Union Square greenmarket the largest in New York. The greenmarket-organization also operates a few stands, with information about composting, organic gardening and healthy cooking. There is also a site where people can leave their organic kitchen waste and discarded textiles.

Inspired by the success of the greenmarkets, in 2008 the city launched the 'Green Cart initiative.' The goal was to promote healthier eating and to combat obesity by licensing 1000 vendors to sell fruits and vegetables in the streets of the poorer neighborhoods. It turned out to be more difficult than expected. Of the 561 vendors who obtained a license in the first year, 60 % threw in the towel. They just couldn't make ends meet. Their problems were the same as those of many other vendors: too much competition, trouble with shopkeepers, theft, rain, heath and cold, a lack of customers, cops who are ill-informed about the complex regulations they are supposed to enforce, too many hours lost in transportation between home, suppliers, the storage of their cart and the place where they sell. And the Green Cart sellers are on their own, unlike the greenmarket sellers who at least have a strong, enthusiastic organization behind them.

VEAL HEART
SATAY

In the Middle East it's called shish kebab, in Indonesia satay, in Greece souvlaki. The Peruvians call it anticuchos. Anticuchos de corazón!

(L) —Manhattan: Union Square
($) 0   5   10   15
(A) —Address n° 24

INGREDIENTS

- 4 cloves garlic, mashed
- 3 tbsp. fresh cilantro, finely chopped
- 3 tbsp. cumin powder
- 3 dried chili peppers, soaked in water, de-seeded, finely chopped
- 1 tsp. salt
- 1 tsp. white pepper
- ¾ cup + 2 tbsp. red wine vinegar
- ⅓ cup + 2 tbsp. vegetable oil
- 2 pounds beef heart
- 20 satay sticks, soaked in water for 30 minutes

STEP BY STEP!

\# In a mortar, add cilantro, cumin, chili, salt and pepper and mash everything into a smooth paste. Add vinegar and ⅓ cup + 2 tbsp. oil. Pour this marinade on the beef, arranged on a plate. Let rest for 30 minutes tops.

\# Remove the meat and set aside the marinade.

\# Thread the meat onto the satay sticks (about 4 pieces a skewer).

\# Brush the marinade onto the meat and grill on a hot grill pan or charcoal grill for about 30 seconds. Turn, brush on more marinade and grill for another 30 seconds.

\# Serve with black mint sauce (see p. 137).

* THERE'S MORE *

This is often served with a boiled potato, with salad and nixtamal (boiled corn) or a piece of bread at the end of the skewer.

BLACK MINT SAUCE

Delicious with skewers!

* THERE'S MORE *

*There are hundreds
of kinds of mint.
Black mint
is a variation of peppermint
and has a very strong taste.
Sometimes it's incorrectly
called huacatay.
If you don't find black mint,
try using peppermint.*

INGREDIENTS

- 8 oz black mint leaves
- 2 dried red chili peppers, soaked
  for 10 minutes in water
- 8 oz cotija cheese, crumbled
- 3 cloves garlic, coarsely chopped
- ¾ cup of unsweetend condensed milk
- 1 tsp. of lime juice
- salt to taste

STEP BY STEP!

Mix all ingredients in a blender and
add salt to taste.

Serve with grilled meat.

Manhattan: Union Square

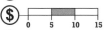
0   5   10   15

Address n° 24

PAPA RELLENA

★ ★

STUFFED POTATO CROQUETTES

This is a dish of which there are many different versions and recipes. From Cuba to Mexico to Peru, everyone has his own interpretation.

STEP BY STEP!

Boil the potatoes till done, about 20 minutes. Use potato masher to mash. Add salt and eggs, let cool and set in refrigerator.

The filling: in a pan add 2 tbsp. vegetable oil, over low heat cook the onion and garlic till soft. Add the beef, turn heat slightly up. Add herbs and season with salt. Let cool.

Put some of the potato mixture, about the size of a large golf ball, in the palm of your hand and make it flat. Add 1 tbsp. of the meat mixture. Close the edges and shape into a ball.

Coat the ball with breadcrumbs and deep fry until golden.

Serve with chili sauce.

(L) — Bronx: Belmont

($) 0   5   10   15

(A) — Address n° 02

INGREDIENTS

- 2 lbs potatoes, peeled
- ¼ tsp. salt
- 2 eggs, slightly beaten
- bread crumbs

Filling
- 2 tbsp. vegetable oil
- 1 onion, finely chopped
- 3 cloves garlic, finely chopped
- 1 pound ground beef chuck
- 1 tsp. cumin powder
- 1 tsp. paprika powder
- ½ tsp. chili powder
- ½ tsp. salt

* THERE'S MORE *

Hard boiled eggs, raisins or olives can all be mixed in the stuffing.

'To die dreaming',
what a beautiful name
for a drink!

(L) —Bronx: Belmont

($) 0 5 10 15

(A) —Address n° 02

MORIR SOÑANDO

>>

Dominican orange milkshake

INGREDIENTS

- 1¼ cups unsweetened
  condensed milk
- 3 tbsp. sugar
- 1 handful ice cubes
- ¾ cup + 2 tbsp. orange juice

STEP BY STEP!

Add the sugar to the milk, stir well.
Cool in refrigerator. Add ice cubes, stir.

Add orange juice, stir well and serve.

* THERE'S MORE *
- - - - - - - - - - - - - - -

*You can use passion fruit juice
instead of orange juice or use half
orange juice, half lime juice.*

*You can use a blender
to make this drink.*

INGREDIENTS

- 4 cups water
- 2 chicken fillets
- 1 tbsp. vegetable oil
- 1 onion, finely chopped
- 1 clove garlic, finely chopped
- 1 tbsp. paprika powder
- ¼ tsp. cumin powder
- ¼ tsp. chili powder
- ¼ tsp. salt
- 8 tortillas
- 2 ¼ cups cheddar cheese, grated

QUESADILLAS

★ ★

Filled tortilla with chicken and cheddar cheese

Queso + tortilla = quesadilla

STEP BY STEP!

\# In a pot bring water to a boil. Turn to low heat and let the chicken briefly simmer till done. Drain, saving the stock in the refrigerator or freezer for later use in soup of other dish. Quickly rinse the chicken under cold water. Shred the meat into fine strips.

\# Heat the vegetable oil in a pan. Fry the onion and garlic till soft. Add paprika, cumin and chili powder.

\# Add the chicken to the pan and season with salt. Remove from the pan and set aside.

\# Place the pan over low heat and add a tortilla. Heap 3 tbsp. chicken mixture on the bottom half of the tortilla. Sprinkle 2 tbsp. cheddar cheese on top. Fold the tortilla and close by pressing the edges together. Cover with lid and bake for 2 minutes. Turn the tortilla, cover again. The tortilla is ready when the cheese is completely melted.

\# Cut the tortilla in three pieces. Serve with a fresh salad with avocado or guacamole.

 Bronx: Columbus Square

0   5   10   15

 Address n° 03

★ ★ ★ ★ ★   ★ ★

Technically, this isn't a real quesadilla but a sincronizada
(Spanish for 'synchronized'). A sincronizada is made with two tortillas
with a cheese based filling in between, while an authentic quesadilla is
made with Oaxaca or other Mexican cheese placed on a tortilla
which is folded in half and grilled or deep-fried.
But the term quesadilla is generally used for any kind of
tortilla-based snack with a cheese-filling.

For the filling, countless variations are possible.
A delectable vegetarian alternative is using mushrooms
instead of chicken. Or you can try a combination of both.

INGREDIENTS

- 2 onions, finely chopped
- 1 clove garlic, finely chopped
- 2 tbsp. vegetable oil
- 1 lb beef, cut in cubes of approximately
  ½ inch by ½ inch
- ½ tsp. cumin powder
- 1 tsp. dried oregano
- 2 tsp. chili powder
- 1 lb cooked rice
- 1 handful fresh cilantro and/or flat-leaf
  Italian parsley, coarsely chopped
- 6- 8 tortillas

Garnish
- guacamole
- sour cream

(L) —Bronx: Columbus Square

($) 0   5   10   15

(A) —Address n° 03

Lucia in The Bronx served
this dish with pride and
insisted that we try it out.
She didn't want us to pay.
But after this culinary feast,
it was a pleasure to stuff
her tip jar.

BEEF BURRITO

STEP BY STEP!

\# Fry one onion and the garlic in 2 tbsp. of oil over low
heat. Add the beef, turn the heat a little higher.
Add cumin, oregon and chili powder.
Fry about 2 minutes till the meat is lightly browned.
Take the meat out of the pan.

\# Add the second onion to the pan. Add additional oil if
desired. Fry over low heat. Add the rice and stir fry for
a few minutes till nicely colored.

\# Add the meat to the rice. Add the cilantro and/or
parsley. Stir briefly and remove from the heat.

\# Place a tortilla on a clean cutting board, spread
5 tbsp. of the meat- and rice mixture on one half. Roll
the tortilla, tuck the outer ridges inside till tightly
closed. Repeat with the remaining tortillas.

\# Preheat the oven to 350 °F. Bake the tortillas for
10 minutes.

\# Serve with guacamole and sour cream.

* THERE'S MORE *

Burrito is also made
with refried beans instead of
or in combination with rice.
After the beans are cooked
and drained they are fried in
oil, bacon or lard. Sometimes
onion and garlic are added.
The fried beans are mashed
till they have the consistency
of mashed potatoes.

(L)—Bronx: Columbus Square

($) 0 5 10 15

(A)—Address n° 03

PORK RIBS
in green sauce ••••••••••••

> The green sauce reminds one of curry but without the complicated herbal mixture.

STEP BY STEP!

\# In a pan add 2 tbsp. vegetable oil and brown the ribs for a few minutes. Remove from the pan.

\# Fry the oil and garlic in the same pan (add a bit more oil if necessary). Add tomatillos and jalapeño peppers, cook until done. Pour water over mixture. Return the ribs to the pan and cook over low heat for approximately 45 minutes till done.

\# Add the cilantro and salt, mix gently.

\# Serve with rice.

INGREDIENTS

- 2 tbsp. vegetable oil
- 2 strips pork ribs, 2 lbs, cut in pieces
- 1 onion, finely chopped
- 2 cloves garlic, finely chopped
- 1 ¼ lbs tomatillos, peeled, coarsely chopped
- 2 jalapeño peppers
- ¾ cup + 2 tbs water
- 1 handful fresh cilantro, finely chopped
- 1 tsp. salt

⁎ THERE'S MORE ⁎

In Mexico tomatillos are sometimes called green tomatoes. They belong to the family of the nightshade, like regular tomatoes, eggplants and bell peppers. The flower of these plants exudes a strong odor, only at night. The green tomato has a sweet sour taste. Combined with chili peppers it forms the base of the popular salsa verde.

POZOLE

Mexican pork soup

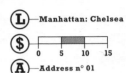

L — Manhattan: Chelsea

$ | 0 5 10 15

A — Address n° 01

> One of my fondest memories of my time in New York: enjoying this dish on the steps of a Mexican church in Chelsea.

INGREDIENTS

- 1 onion, finely chopped
- 2 cloves garlic, peeled and mashed
- 2 tbsp. vegetable oil
- 1 tsp. white pepper
- ½ tsp. oregano
- ½ tsp. chili powder
- ½ tsp. cumin powder
- 1 ¾ lb pork shoulder
- 4 cups water
- 1 ½ lb corn kernels in nixtamal style (cooked, soaked in lime, rinsed and dehulled)
- 2 green chili peppers, finely chopped
- 1 tsp. salt
- 1 bunch fresh cilantro, finely chopped

Garnish
- lime wedges
- chili sauce

STEP BY STEP!

\# In a pot add 2 tbsp. oil and fry onion and garlic. Add pepper, oregano, chili powder and cumin. Add the pork shoulder, add water. Bring to a boil. Let simmer over low heat for 45 minutes. Regularly skim off the foam.

\# Remove the pork shoulder. In a mixing bowl strain the stock through cheesecloth or a kitchen towel to draw out the remaining fat. Pour the stock back in the pot, add the nixtamal corn kernels and bring back to a boil. Let simmer for an hour.

\# Cut the pork shoulder into bit size pieces and add with chili peppers to the stock. Season with salt to taste.

\# Add cilantro to the soup.

This dish goes back
to the time of the Aztecs.
It was eaten
during rituals.

New York, oyster city

Jasper Danckaerts, a Dutchman who in 1679-1680 explored the region of what's now New York, reported that the oysters there were 30 centimeters long (almost 1 foot). According to him, lobsters were more than a meter (3 feet) long and the wild turkeys weighed 20 kilogram (44 pounds). His description of this land of plenty is quoted in Mark Kurlansky's captivating book, *The Big Oyster: History on the Half Shell* (2006).

Until the end of the 1920s oysters were very important for the city, in culinary terms, as well as culturally and economically. Today, there are still enormous quantities of oysters eaten in New York. But they are no longer harvested locally and they're a lot more expensive than before.

The Crassostrea virginica, the prevalent species of oysters along America's east coast, loves the brackish water of river mouths. Oysters used to thrive up to a hundred kilometers (62 miles) upstream the Hudson, in the East River and along the shores of Queens, Brooklyn, Staten Island and New Jersey. There were two small islands in the bay of New York where oysters were so abundant that the Dutch called them Big Oyster Island and Small Oyster Island. Today, they're called Liberty Island (where the statue of Liberty stands) and Ellis Island. Some historians estimate that, at the time when the Dutch founded Nieuw-Amsterdam, the bay of New York contained half of all the oysters in the world.

Before the Europeans arrived, the Indian population consumed large quantities of oysters. This is proven by the mountains of oyster shells which were found at various places in New York, some of them dating back to 6950 BC. The first Europeans here just had to walk to the shore to pick up a portion of oysters. Later, boats were used to harvest them. In many streets of old New York there were oyster cellars, recognized by the red light above the entrance. You could buy cheap oysters there and patronize cheap prostitutes. On just about every street corner there was an oyster stall. The vendors grilled, braised, and fried, the mollusks. Lovers of raw oysters bought them at colorful outdoor markets like the Fulton and Washington Market.

Oysters were so cheap that it was said the poor of New York ate nothing but oysters and bread. In the 19th century, restaurants offered a 'Canal Street plan,' named thusly for the many oyster cellars in Canal Street. For 6 cents, customers could fill their bellies with oysters. Yet the rich also loved oysters. They were on the menu for copious banquets and posh restaurants. The New York oysters were so good that they were in high demand as far as San Francisco and London. They were so famous that, when someone departed for New York, the goodbyes were often accompanied with the shout: 'Enjoy the oysters!'

But those delicious New York oysters were so greedily consumed that the oyster banks were threatened with depletion by the start of the 19th century. To prevent this, oyster seeds and young oysters were brought over from the more southern Chesapeake Bay. Often, it was free blacks from this region who did the replanting of New York's oysters banks. Many of them decided to stay because they felt more free than in Virginia and Maryland where they came from. They found work, not only as fishermen but also as oyster-vendors and keepers of oyster cellars.

Pollution sounded the death knell for New York's oysters. Raw sewage and industrial waste were dumped in the water untreated. In 1927 the city decided to close the last oyster bank in Staten Island's Raritan Bay.

Since then, New York has morphed into a post-industrial city. The water in and around it is again clean enough for oysters. For now, the oyster farming is still in an experimental stage.

The oysters are doing well but are still not suitable for consumption. There are still too many PCBs and heavy metals in the water. But the oysters themselves are helping to clean the water. There is another reason to bring back the oyster banks. They function as a buffer against storms. That there is a need for this was made quite clear by the wreckage caused by super storm Sandy in October 2012. Not that the oyster banks by themselves could have prevented this, but they could become a part of the defense which the city needs against future storms.

The day that oysters from New York are back on the menu is still far off. In the meantime, New Yorkers and visitors to the city enjoy oysters harvested along the shores of Long Island, Rhode Island, Maine and Prince Edward Island (Canada). In the Oyster Bar, a famous, by now hundred year-old restaurant, in the vaulted basement of Grand Central Terminal, there are often more than 30 kinds of oysters on the menu, as well as the tasty **oyster roast pan**. In the Lobster Place, an attractive fish store in Chelsea Market, the assortment is equally large. And in markets like Smorgasborg in Williamsburg (Brooklyn) and the New Amsterdam Market at South Street Seaport, skillful boys and girls open the oysters in front of your eyes and you can slurp the delicacy standing up, like in old New York.

Cosenza's
OYSTER
BAR

COSENZA'S
FISH MARKET
2394 Arthur Ave, Bronx, N.Y.
(718) 364-8510

OYSTER
PAN ROAST

Once, local oysters were abundant in New York.
They were used in many different dishes.

INGREDIENTS

- 8 to 10 fresh oysters
- 2 tbsp. butter
- 2 tbsp. oyster- or clam juice
- 1 tbsp. chili sauce
- 1 tsp. Worcestershire sauce
- dash of celery salt to taste
- ½ cup cream
- 2 slices crusty bread, toasted, diagonally cut into points
- 1 tsp. butter
- sweet paprika

L—Manhattan: Grand Central

A—Address n° 10

STEP BY STEP!

In a sauce pan melt butter, add oysters. Add oyster or clam juice, chili sauce, Worcestershire sauce and celery salt.

Stir well, heat till the mixture simmers and the edges of the oysters start to curl.

Add cream, bring back to a simmer.

Arrange toast points in a serving bowl and pour the oyster mixture on top. Add some butter and paprika to taste.

Serve immediately.

∗ THERE'S MORE ∗

In New York's Grand Central Oyster Bar individual oyster pan roasts are still made every day in the original way; which means in the same way as when the restaurant opened in 1913.

PEANUTS 1.50
COCONUTS 2.00
ALMONDS 2.50
CASHEWS 2.50
MIX 3.00

The Pickle Guys
www.pickleguys.com
PICKLES ON ST STREET SINCE 1910
NEW YORK, NY

NUTS 4 NUTS

NYC Love
STREET COFFEE
www.nyclovec...

Janna

the BEST Soul Fo[od]
[N]YC Since 1984

The sweet potato is nutritious. It can be cooked, deep-fried or baked. It can be made into puree, soup, curry dishes or pastry. It's traditionally served on Thanksgiving.

Ⓛ —**Manhattan: Harlem**

Ⓢ

0	5	10	15

Ⓐ —**Address n° 04**

INGREDIENTS

- 2 medium sized yams
- fleur de sel or kosher salt
- black pepper, freshly ground
- butter

STEP BY STEP!

Preheat the oven to 400 °F. Prick the yam all over with a fork.

Bake the yam for 1 hour or until soft. Check with a fork if the yam is done. The fork should slide easily with little resistance.

Cut lengthwise and serve with salt, black pepper and butter to taste.

Serve with collard greens (see p. 160) or with macaroni and cheese (see p. 167)

Tip: yams can also be cooked in the microwave. Important: first prick the yam all over with a fork.

YAMS
Sweet potatoes

///

Americans often call their sweet potatoes yams, although technically, they aren't. The real yam is grown in Africa and Asia and is more mealy and dry than the American sweet potato. At first sight, they look alike. That explains why the African slaves called sweet potatoes yams. The two names are still used as synonyms, so we do that too. Yams are a basic ingredient in soul food cuisine, which likes to emphasize the sweetness of the tubers by adding brown sugar. There are two kinds of sweet potatoes: one is more dry and hard, the other is softer and sweeter.

INGREDIENTS

- 1 medium onion, chopped
- ¼ cup olive oil
- 2 cloves garlic
- 8 cups water
- 1 lb smoked meat (ham hock, bacon
  or turkey wings or necks)
- 1 tbsp. Tabasco sauce
- 1 tsp. salt
- 3 large bushels collard greens, you may also use kale,
  rapini, beet greens, mustard greens, turnip greens,
  Swiss chard or spinach (the last two cook faster)
- 1 tbsp. butter

Ⓛ—Manhattan: Harlem

Ⓢ— 0 5 10 15

Ⓐ—Address n° 04

COLLARD GREENS *Boerenkool*

★ ★

In the southern states of the US it's an old custom to give green vegetables more taste with ham hocks and other smoked or salted pork. Contemporary cooks increasingly prefer smoked turkey wings and necks because the meat is less fatty. So collard greens, a typical soul food dish, can be prepared with either pork or turkey meat.

STEP BY STEP!

In a sauté pan fry the onion in the olive oil for 2 minutes. Stir a couple of times with a wooden spoon. Add the garlic. Fry for about 1 to 2 minutes, stir, making sure the garlic doesn't brown. Add 8 cups of water together with the meat, Tabasco sauce, salt and bring to a boil. Let simmer for about 1 hour.

Rinse the greens well.
Remove the stems and membranes, except from the young leaves.

Layer 6 to 9 collard green leaves on top of each other and roll up. Cut into ½ inch pieces.

Add to the meat together with the butter. Cover. Let simmer for 45 to 60 minutes, stirring occasionally.

Take the meat out of the pot, remove the bone. Shred the meat and add again to the greens, stir well. Season to taste.

Collard greens are of the same family as
broccoli and cabbage.
They are also eaten in Brazil, Portugal,
the Balkans, Africa and India.

Collard greens with black-eyed peas
and corn bread (recipe, see p. 168)
is a typical new year's dish
in the soul food cuisine.

The dish is supposed to bring luck
because the rolled up green leaves
resemble rolls of dollar bills.

The corn bread is used to sop up
the cooking juice of the collard greens,
which is very nutritious.
Some people add 1 tablespoon of sugar
to the cooking water before putting
the vegetable in it.
Before serving, some add
a bit of pepper and vinegar.

OKRA AND TOMATOES

★ ★

Okra originally is a tropical plant with edible legumes that are eaten in North and South America, the Middle East and Africa. It's an essential ingredient in soul food, the cuisine of southern blacks.

★ ★

STEP BY STEP!

\# Sauté garlic, onion and green pepper in oil about 10 minutes or until the vegetables are tender. Add remaining ingredients, and cook 5 minutes, stirring frequently.

Ⓛ —Manhattan: Harlem

Ⓢ — 0   5   10   15

Ⓐ —Address n° 04

INGREDIENTS

- 1 clove garlic, minced
- ½ cup onion, chopped
- ½ cup green pepper, chopped
- 2 tbsp. olive oil
- 2 cups okra, sliced
- 3 cups tomatoes, peeled and sliced
- ¼ tsp. dried oregano
- salt and black pepper to taste

* THERE'S MORE *

Okra is rich in fibers, vitamine B and C, anti-oxidants, calcium and potassium. Because the entire plant is edible, there are many ways to prepare it. The legumes can be deep-fried or stir fried. They can be stuffed and baken in the oven. The legumes and leaf are used in soups and stews like gumbo, the famous Louisiana dish. The roasted seeds are even said to be an acceptable substitute for coffee.

MACARONI & CHEESE *Soul food delight*

///

Mac & cheese is one of America's comfort foods, the kind that goes down easily and reminds people of their childhood. It's a popular dish with young and old.
It is also associated with the Southern states of the US.
The dish is often served at barbecues and is always on the menu in soul food restaurants.

INGREDIENTS

- 1 8 oz package macaroni pasta
- 3 tbsp. butter
- 3 tbsp. flour
- 3 cups milk
- 1 tsp. coarse salt (kosher or sea salt)
- ½ tsp. paprika
- 1 bay leaf
- black pepper, freshly ground
- 1 egg
- 2 ½ cups sharp cheddar, grated

For the finish:
- 3 tbsp. butter
- 1 cup bread crumbs

STEP BY STEP!

Heat the oven to 350 °F.

In a large pot of boiling salted water, cook the pasta to al dente.

In another large pot melt the butter over medium heat, add the flour. Use a whisk to stir till the mixture is free of lumps. Slowly add the milk. Keep stirring till the mixture has thickened.

Add salt, paprika, bay leaf and black pepper. Keep stirring for about 5 minutes over low heat. Remove the bay leaf.

In a small bowl temper the egg with a bit of sauce. Add the mixture and three quarts of the cheese to the rest of the sauce. Stir. Fold the macaroni into the sauce and pour into a greased 2- quart casserole dish. Scatter the remaining cheese on top of the macaroni.

Melt the remaining butter in a sauté pan and toss the bread crumbs to coat. Top the macaroni with the crumbs. Bake for 30 minutes.

* THERE'S MORE *

Some cooks add a finely chopped onion. Others use a mixture of sharp cheeses. Some like to flavor the sauce with beer or even truffle oil.

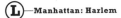
Ⓛ —Manhattan: Harlem

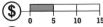
Ⓢ 0   5   10   15

Ⓐ —Address n° 04

CORNBREAD

>>>>>>>>>>>>>>>>>>>>>>>>>>> ★ <<<<<<<<<<<<<<<<<<<<<<<<<<<<<<<

Cornbread is an important staple in the cuisine of the Southern states of the US. Corn has been the basic food for native Americans for thousands of years. The colonists in the South learned to use it as a substitute for wheat. Corn bread can be baked, steamed or deep-fried. It can have different names, depending on how it's prepared: corn pone, johnny cakes, hush puppies, baked cornbread or hot water cornbread.

INGREDIENTS

- 4 oz flour
- 1 tbsp. baking powder
- ½ tsp. salt
- 6 oz cornmeal
- 1 tbsp. sugar
- 2 eggs
- 1 cup milk
- 2/3 cup vegetable oil

STEP BY STEP!

Preheat the oven to 400 °F.

In a bowl mix the flour, baking powder, salt, cornmeal and sugar.
In a separate bowl blend eggs, milk and oil. Add to the flour mix and blend till smooth.

Pour the dough in a greased 10 inch square pan. Bake for 20 minutes till golden brown.

* THERE'S MORE *

Usually, cornbread is less sweet of in the South than in the North. Cornbread is often used as stuffing for the Thanksgiving-turkey. It's a staple in soul food restaurants and cafeterias. It is perfect with a zesty barbecue, chili con carne and stew pots.

Hearty versions of cornbread are made by adding bits of bacon, jalapeño peppers, scallions, cheese, cumin or cracklings (pieces of roasted or deep-fried pork skin).

Buttermilk can be used instead of regular milk. Creamed corn kernels can be added to the batter.

WELCOME TO
ANNA'S
.99/Lb.
.99/Lb.
only MEAT

L — Manhattan: Harlem

$ — 0 5 10 15

A — Address n° 04

→ continuation of p. 129

Jacqueline invites us to stay at her house. Since it would make our work easier and we get along fine, we move from Brooklyn's Red Hook to her place in Staten Island. It's a beautiful Sunday when Jacqueline takes us along to West 14th Street. There, right in front of the church, is a weekly culinary feast. A Mexican family prepares delicious tacos. In an improvised stand, surrounded by cardboard and under an umbrella with the misleading lettering 'soft pretzels,' there are large bowls of broth and plastic pots filled with salsa. The eldest son suggests that we try the **pozole**. That is a soup of a nice, fat broth containing slowly cooked pork meat, served with a slice of lime and homemade chili sauce. The combination of all these ingredients is as simple as it is delicious. With my limited Spanish and the help of the boy's iPhone, I find out the composition of this unique dish. Pozole goes back to the Aztecs who served it at their ceremonies. The guy is visibly pleased that we love his soup so much. The rich taste of the chili sauce reflects the love and patience that went into its preparation. Our pleasant conversation and the discovery of this soup leave me with a warm feeling of simple happiness.

We look for the closest subway station and take a train to Harlem's 125th Street. Here I discover soul food. We enter a cafeteria called Manna's. Jacqueline and I each compose a meal at the buffet table. The offer of nicely presented dishes on aluminum trays looks pretty under the hot yellow bulbs. **Yams, collard greens, okra and tomato, macaroni & cheese** and a piece of **cornbread** color our plates. We take our styrofoam boxes outside and install ourselves on a bench in the nearby Marcus Garvey park. A few locals growl approvingly when they see our takeout meals. Once again, our eyes were bigger than our stomachs. There's no way we can eat all this delicious stuff. Jacqueline packs all that remains neatly so that her friend at home can enjoy the harvest of our street food raid as well.

Some time later, Jacqueline presents us to Veronica, an elderly Jamaican lady with a great smile, who sells her soul food dishes from a food cart downtown, near Wall Street Plaza. Veronica lets us taste from her spicy **oxtail stew**. She makes me guess which spices she has used. She serves her dishes in hamburger boxes. We also taste her **jerk chicken** and beans & rice with homemade chili sauce. What a party in our mouths! I order **sorrel**, a refreshing homemade lemonade, in which I recognize a hint of cinnamon.

The Bistro truck is parked a bit further. There, Luk orders a **vegetarian tajin**. Jacqueline has a hankering for Greek and goes to the Souvlaki truck for a plate of **Greek skewers** and a fresh **feta salad**. On less than a hundred square meters, we have tasted three world cuisines.

→ continues on p. 192

- 2 lbs oxtail, cut in pieces
- 2 tbsp. butter
- 2 tbsp. vegetable oil
- 4 onions, finely chopped
- 3 carrots
- 1 green pepper, finely chopped
- 2 cloves garlic, finely chopped
- 1 tbsp. paprika powder
- 1 tbsp. salt
- 4 sprigs fresh thyme
- 2 tbsp. allspice
- ½ tsp. cinnamon powder
- 1 tsp. nutmeg, ground
- ½ tsp. ginger powder

- 2 tbsp. Jamaican browning sauce
- 4 cups water
- 4 cloves

Jamaican browning sauce:
- 2 ½ cups chicken- or beef stock
- ¾ cups + 2 tbsp. soy sauce
- ¾ cups + 2 tbsp. dry sherry
- 1 cup brown sugar
- 4 cloves
- 2 star anise
- 1 inch piece of fresh ginger,
  peeled and mashed

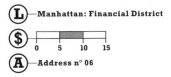

L—Manhattan: Financial District

$ 0 5 10 15

A—Address n° 06

OXTAIL STEW

OXTAIL IS A VERY TASTY PIECE OF MEAT IF YOU LET IT STEW FOR A LONG TIME OVER LOW HEAT.

\# In a saucepan with heavy bottom, add all browning sauce ingredients and bring to a boil over low heat. Let thicken for about 30 minutes, set aside.

\# Remove the excessive fat from the oxtail. Clean and rinse under cold water.

\# In a pan add 2 tbsp. butter over medium heat. Brown the oxtail on all sides. Remove from the pan and set aside.

\# Heat the oil in a second pan and cook the onion till soft. Add carrots, peppers and garlic, cook for a few more minutes.

\# Add paprika powder, salt, thyme, allspice, cinnamon powder, nutmeg and ginger powder. Blend everything well, add oxtail and Jamaican browning sauce. Add 4 cups of water and bring gently to a boil. Cover. Let simmer for 2 ½ hours over low heat, gently stirring the sauce occasionally.

\# Serve over rice.

JERK
CHICKEN

So roasted ◆

◆ ◆ ◆ ◆ ◆ ◆ ◆ ◆ ◆ ◆ ◆

◆ ◆ ◆ ◆ ◆ ◆ ◆ ◆ ◆ ◆

◆ ◆ ◆ ◆ ◆ ◆ ◆ ◆ ◆ ◆

◆ ◆

'Jerk' is a typical Jamaican recipe and refers to the herb mixture that is used as well as to the cooking method. This recipe can be made on a grill or in the oven.

STEP BY STEP!

\# Cut the chicken in half and cut further into smaller pieces. Put the meat in a bowl and add lime juice. Let rest for 1 hour.

\# Prepare the marinade. Pound the dried herbs fine in a mortar. Add the onion, Scotch Bonnet pepper and thyme and pound further into a smooth paste.

\# Mix the paste with vinegar, olive oil and rum.

\# Rub the herb mixture all over the chicken pieces. Let marinade for at least 2 hours.

\# Preheat the oven grill to 400 °F. Arrange the chicken in a oven dish, skin side up. Pour the marinade around the meat.

\# Turn the chicken pieces after 15 minutes, baste again with the marinade. Turn the chicken two more times, baste each time with marinade till done to taste.

INGREDIENTS

- 1 medium sized chicken
- ⅓ cup + 2 tbsps. lime juice

Marinade
- 2 tbsp. allspice
- 1 ½ tbsp. sugar
- 1 ½ tbsp. salt
- 1 tsp. black pepper
- ⅓ tsp. cinnamon powder
- ½ tsp. ginger powder
- 3 onions, coarsely chopped
- 6 gloves garlic, coarsely chopped
- 2 Scotch Bonnet-peppers (habanero peppers), seeded and coarsely chopped (or use jalapeño peppers)
- 4 sprigs thyme
- ⅓ cup vinegar
- ⅓ cup olive oil
- 2 tbsp. brown rum

Ⓛ —Manhattan: Financial District

$ |___|▓▓|___|___|
   0   5   10   15

Ⓐ —Address n° 06

★ ★ ★ ★ ★ ★ ★ ★ ★ ★   ★ ★

Allspice is a typical spice
of Caribbean cuisine.
The fruit or berry resembles
pepper but it has the aroma
of cloves, nutmeg, cinnamon
and ginger.
The bush on which
these berries grow is called
pimenta by the Spanish.

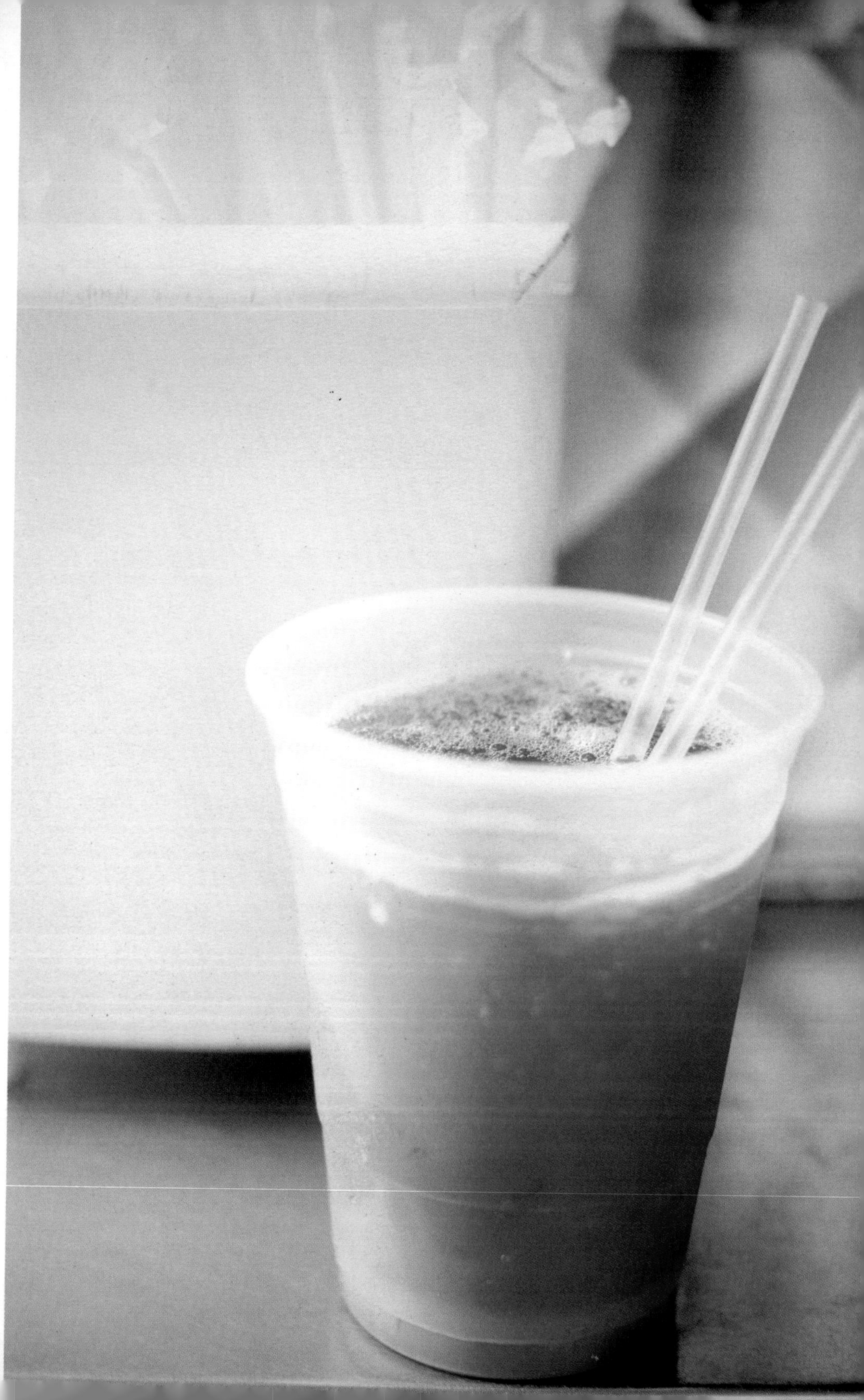

Ⓛ —Manhattan: Financial District

Ⓢ 0 5 10 15

Ⓐ —Address n° 06

SORREL

Lemonade of the rosella flower

I tasted this first at Veronica's Kitchen, Jamaican food in the Financial District. Later I discovered that this flower grows in Asia and Africa as well and is used there too for making drinks.

* THERE'S MORE *

Don't confuse the flower sorrel (rosella) with the green and sour tasting sorrel plant. It is the flower which is used for the drink.

Adding a piece of ginger to the mix gives the drink a stronger flavor. Or you could mix ginger beer with the sorrel.

INGREDIENTS

- 12 cups water
- 8 oz Jamaican sorrel
- 1 cup sugar
- 1 cinnamon stick
- 5 cloves
- 1 chunk of fresh ginger, 1 to 2 inches according to taste, peeled (optional)
- 1 lime
- water

STEP BY STEP!

\# In a pot, bring the water to a boil. While the water boils add the sorrel, sugar, cinnamon stick, cloves and ginger (if used).

\# Turn off the heat, cover and let rest overnight.

\# Strain the lemonade and add more sugar and lime juice according to taste. Add some water if a less strong flavor is preferred.

\# Serve chilled.

You can add all kinds of vegetables to the boiling mixture in the tajine: chickpeas, beans, bell peppers, tomatoes... But beware, keep the different cooking times of the vegetables in mind. You might consider letting a pickled lemon boil along. It gives a fresh touch.

In a bowl, add the couscous, pour vegetable stock on it. Let rest for 20 minutes to let the couscous absorb the liquid. Fluff with a fork and add the almond slivers, toss gently.

In the tajine (traditional North African earth ware slow cooker) add 2 tbps vegetable oil, onion and garlic. Stir. Add all the herbs and half of the vegetable stock.

Put the lid on the tajine, let the vegetables steam for at least 15 minutes. Add more vegetable stock and extra herbs, if desired.

Serve on top of the couscous and with a fresh salad.

- 2 tbsp. vegetable oil
- 2 onions, finely chopped
- 2 cloves garlic, mashed
- 3 potatoes, peeled and
  cut into ¾ inch chunks
- 1 zucchini, halved and
  cut into ½ inch slices
- 3 carrots, scraped, cut into ½ inch pieces
- ½ butternut squash, peeled, seeded,
  cut into ¾ inch chunks
- 1 tsp. ginger powder
- 1 tsp. white pepper, ground
- 1 tsp. paprika powder
- 1 tsp. cumin powder
- 1 tsp. ras el hanout
- 1 tsp. turmeric powder
- 1 tsp. salt
- 1. ¼ cups vegetable stock
- 1 eggplant, halved, cut into ½ inch slices

Couscous
- 1 lb couscous
- 2 ½ cups vegetable stock
- 2 oz almond slivers, roasted

Ⓛ —Manhattan: Financial District

$

| 0 | 5 | 10 | 15 |

Ⓐ —Address n° 07

VEGETABLE TAJINE WITH COUSCOUS

★ ★

FROM THE MEDITERRANEAN AND NORTH AFRICAN CUISINE.

GREEK CHICKEN SKEWERS

SOUVLAKI

In a bar at the edge of Chinatown I met Paul who used to operate the Souvlaki GR truck. When I expressed my passion for street food, he served me souvlaki with fries, feta cheese and rosemary. The chicken skewers were juicy and delectably seasoned.

INGREDIENTS

- 2 lbs chicken fillets
- 1 tbsp. dried oregano
- 3 cloves garlic, mashed
- some black olives
- 1 tsp. salt
- ½ tsp. black pepper
- 4 tbsp. olive oil
- 4 tbsp. lime juice
- 2 tbsp. red wine vinegar
- 15 wooden satay skewers, soaked in water for 30 minutes

STEP BY STEP!

\# Cut the chicken in to 2 inch by 2 inch pieces. Add the meat and all ingredients to a bowl. Let marinate for 2 hours.

\# Remove the chicken from the marinade. Put 3 to 4 pieces on each skewer.

\# Heat a grill pan and grill the chicken skewers for about 3 to 4 minutes on each side.

\# Serve with feta salad (see p. 183), some black olives and tzatziki.

* THERE'S MORE *

Instead of chicken, you can use pork, beef or lamb. Souvlaki is often served on pita bread.

L—Manhattan: Financial District

$ 0 5 10 15

A—Address n° 08

Between 1950 and 1970 many Greeks settled in and around New York. At the peak of their immigration, Greeks owned more than 600 diners in the New York area. Other Greeks had souvlaki stands. Salad of feta cheese, cucumber and tomato was always on the menu. Meanwhile Greek feta, as well as similar white cheeses from countries like Bulgaria, Turkey and Albania, are well established in New York.

Ⓛ —**Manhattan: Financial District**
Ⓢ
Ⓐ —**Address n° 08**

0   5   10   15

Feta cheese, cucumber and tomato salad

VERY REFRESHING AND READY IN NO TIME

Nothing is more refreshing on a typical subtropical New York summer evening than a delicious salad of feta cheese, cucumber and tomato. The dish is ready in a jiffy.

STEP BY STEP!

Cut the tomatoes in slices.

Cut the cucumber length wise. Remove seeds if desired. Cut into ½ inch pieces.

Add the vinegar, olive oil, feta and mint or oregano to the tomatoes and cucumber. Toss well.

For variation: add slices red onion, black olives, green, red or green peppers, any salad greens of a handful of croutons.

Help

→ continuation of p. 099

Sean Basinski became a fan of street food while he traveled through Asia and Africa before commencing his studies. Back in New York he started his own Mexican food stand. He thought it would be a fun way to make some money for college. But it soon became clear to him that he had seriously underestimated how hard it would be. It was that same scorching summer of 1998 when Mayor Giuliani decreed his prohibition. Sean was very active in organizing the resistance to it. Later, after he finished law school, he received a grant to set up a project for people who lacked access to the judicial system. He immediately thought about New York's street vendors who had no professional organization, no aid from lawyers or interpreters. That was the start of the Street Vendor Project in 2002. The organization shares the 16th floor of a building downtown with 75 people who work for the Urban Justice Center. It defends the rights of New York's most vulnerable inhabitants including homeless people, mental patients, prostitutes and LGTB-youngsters -- and street vendors.

The Street Vendor Project (SVP) focuses on all street vendors, from hotdog sellers to sunglass peddlers. In exchange for a modest membership fee (100 dollar a year) they receive help with problems with licenses, fines and access to stands. SVP distributes information about the regulations in five languages. In 2012 the organization won a court case against the city. The city's practice of imposing exorbitant fines for small infractions was condemned. The judge ordered the city to pay back 228,000 dollars immediately and to reduce outstanding fines of 4 million dollars.

In 2004 the SVP launched the Vendy Awards, a kind of Grammy Awards for the best street food. The public and a jury chose their favorites in different categories. The Vendy Awards have become popular yearly events, not only in New York but also in Los Angeles and Philadelphia. Part of the proceeds go to the Street Vendor Project. The winners get media attention and lots of curious customers.

Thomas De Geest, the Belgian owner of Wafels & Dinges, won in 2009 in the category 'dessert'. He is considered to be one of the most successful entrepreneurs among the street food vendors. He is not a member of the SVP, but of the New York City Food Truck Association (NYCFA). Founded in 2011, the NYCFA represents 45 of the more than 70 food truck owners in New York. The food trucks are a relatively new phenomenon. The first ones started to cruise the city in 2007. They were an instant hit. The trucks have more room to cook and stock supplies so they can offer a greater variety of dishes. The food truck owners are the big boys among the street food vendors. Their organization, the NYCFA, has enough money to hire a lobbyist who negotiates with the different city agencies about things like parking rules and licenses. The much less moneyed Street Vendor Project can only dream of such things but hopefully its members, with their modest stalls and carts, can benefit from it as well.

Street Vendor Project, www.streetvendor.org
New York City Food Truck Association, www.nycfoodtrucks.org

Behind the scenes
at Wafels & Dinges

Thomas De Geest started Wafels & Dinges in 2007. In the beginning, he did all the work himself. By 2013 he was the owner of two new food trucks, five food carts and a store in the East Village. He employs 60 people.

We arranged to meet on an early Saturday morning in the industrial part of Brooklyn where his commissary is located. It's still dark when I drive onto the desolated street. Despite the biting wind, the gates of Wafels & Dinges are wide open. It's five to six. Thomas greets me, wrapped in a warm coat and a cap of the same yellow color in which his trucks and carts are painted. 'This is the night shift,' he says, pointing to two women and five men who are intensely focused on their work. 'They have cleaned the trucks and the carts and are now stocking them.' De Geest, who's Belgian, gave his equipment names, mostly typically Flemish ones. The two trucks are called Big ol' Momma and Kastaar. The food carts were baptized Bierbeek, Kotmadam, Goesting, Vedette and Pagadder. Thomas invites me to look at Goesting ('Appetite'). There is not a speck to be seen on the stainless steel interior. The waffle irons are perfectly scrubbed. White buckets filled with batter, as well as coffee, chocolate milk, bananas, strawberries, whipped cream, 'spekuloos' spread, dulce de leche, ice cream and Nutella are neatly stacked in the cleverly organized cart.

'My night shift people are fantastic,' Thomas says. 'They're all Mexicans, hard workers.' Thomas speaks with them in fluent Spanish. 'My wife is from Venezuela,' he explains.
I ask him if his employees have health insurance. 'They can have it', he says, 'if they pay 200 dollars per month. That's 70% of the premium and I pay the rest. But if they have a family, it costs them 800 dollars per month.' For the Mexicans of the night shift it's an impossibly high amount. They earn 8 dollars an hour – exactly the price of a **waffle with chile con corne** – and that's just 75 cent more than the legal minimum wage in the US. In New York, where the costs of living are high, 14 dollars an hour is considered a livable minimum wage. But even with that, a family covering health insurance would remain unreachable. No health insurance at all is the rule in New York's street food industry. In part because of this, the prices are so low and companies like Wafels & Dinges are successful.

I get the tour of the workspace. The first thing that strikes me is how clean and well organized everything is. There is an office behind a glass wall with workspace for five people. 'One of them just handles the catering,' says Thomas. At parties, Wafels & Dinges treats the guests with fresh waffles in Brussels or Liège style. 'A customer can call us and if he wishes, we'll be there in two to three hours. Because we're fast, we have a good reputation in the film industry. Just the other day Alec Baldwin called us because he wanted to treat the set that same day. No problem.' Before we leave the office, Thomas points to two papers on the notice-board: recent fines. One for 1000 dollars, the other 2000. In both cases, something was wrong with the seller's license of one of the employees of a waffle cart. Three thousand dollars, that's a lot of waffles. 'The city is unreasonable,' Thomas says, 'but what can I do but pay?'

Next to the office, there is the spacious white-tiled kitchen area. A girl and two men are making the batter for the Liège style waffles. Flower, butter, yeast, vanilla-extract, egg yolk, salt, water and Belgian pearl sugar, are meticulously weighed before they are mixed in a kneading machine imported from Germany. I'm also shown the huge refrigerators and freezers where the stocks are. In a corner near the entrance there is a small shop where one

can buy T-shirts, and spekuloos (ginger bread) cookies and spread. 'That's for when we do tours', Thomas says. Meanwhile, it's 7 am. The sun has just risen. The four carts and trucks have left for their stands. They open every day at 8 am. Some stay open until after 10 pm. Then they have to return to the commissary in Brooklyn where the Mexican night shift will once again clean and stock the whole fleet so that it can hit the road again by 7 am.

WAFELS & DINGES

Good Things Belgian

Wall Street

2 3

WAFFLE WITH CHILI CON CORNE

◆◆◆◆◆◆◆◆◆◆◆◆◆◆◆◆◆◆◆◆◆◆◆◆◆◆◆◆◆◆◆◆◆◆◆

New Yorkers discovered Belgian waffles at the New York World's Fair of 1964. Back then, a waffle with whipped cream and strawberries cost 1 dollar. The Belgian waffle became a success. America began to eat waffles for breakfast and as dessert, often with ice cream and strawberries or another soft fruit, for example banana. Half a century later food trucks in cities like Portland, Austin and New York were delighting their customers with new, daring hearty waffle recipes like the vegetarian chili con corne of Wafels & Dinges. The name 'corne' is a wink to the classic chili con carne and also refers to the corn meal that is used in this vegetarian recipe.

STEP BY STEP!

WAFELS

\# In a large mixing bowl, mix the dry ingredients.
Mix the wet ingredients, corn included, in another bowl.

\# Mix wet with dry ingredients. Add 1 tsp. baking powder.

\# Grease the waffle iron with the butter. Bake each waffle for about 4 minutes.

CHILI

\# Bring the vegetable stock to a boil. Add the bulgur and bring back to a boil. Cover and let simmer for 15 minutes. Remove from the heat when the bulgur is done. Fluff the bulgur with a fork, cover again. Let rest for 8 minutes.

\# In a crock-pot, add tomatoes, corn and beans. Set on high.
Add bulgur.

\# In a large skillet, heat the oil. Add onion, cumin and chili powder. Fry the onion till soft, add the green peppers and garlic. Fry for another 2 to 3 minutes.

\# Add the onion, green peppers and garlic to the crock-pot. Cover and heat 10 to 30 minutes on maximum temperature.

\# Turn on low, let cook covered for several hours till done.

\# Serve each waffle with a chili portion on top. Garnish with 1 to 2 tbsp. sour cream or Greek yogurt and some chopped fresh cilantro.

INGREDIENTS

for 40 waffles
- 3 cups flour
- 10 cups yellow corn meal
- 2 cups brown sugar
- 8 tsp. salt
- 2 tsp. black pepper
- 2 tsp. chili powder
- 4 tsp. cumin powder
- 8 cups ½ heavy cream and ½ milk
- 2 cups whole eggs
- 1 cup canola oil
- 3 cups drained corn kernels
- 1 tsp. baking powder
- butter at the ready to grease waffle iron

for the vegetarian chili
- 1 cup clear vegetable stock
- 5 oz bulgur
- 1½ lbs tomatoes
- 2 cups corn
- 1 8oz can black beans (rinsed and drained)
- 1 8oz can red beans (rinsed and drained)
- 3 tbsp. olive oil
- 1 lb chopped onion
- 1 tsp. cumin powder
- 3 tsp. chili powder
- 2 green peppers, finely chopped
- 3 cloves garlic, minced
- sour cream or Greek yogurt
- fresh cilantro, freshly chopped

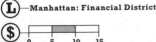

(L)—Manhattan: Financial District

($)

0   5   10   15

(A)—Address n° 11

→ continuation of p. 170

We follow Jacqueline through Vinegar Hill in Brooklyn. Vinegar Hill is the place in New York where 'slow cooking' originated. Many cooks with long beards can be admired here in their open kitchens, like living sign boards of this movement. We saunter through Dumbo, a convivial artistic neighborhood where an Arts Festival is going on. We stand in line for pizza at Grimaldi's. In the South Bronx, on 152nd and Wales Street, we visit some crazy Puerto Ricans who are visibly happy to see us. They are in a party mood and we don't even have to pay for the **empanada** they give us. Rock & Roll street food vendors! No fancy truck for them, they use a worn out gypsy cart, in which you can sit while waiting for your order. The atmosphere is friendly and ebullient. Too bad that places like this are disappearing. I wonder how long this one will survive. The ever more stringent inspections and increasing fines are putting a damper on the creativity and the spontaneous, cordial character of such places.

We enjoy a **chicken tikka** at a food truck in Harlem and Jacqueline leads us through Columbia University and Morningside Heights Park to 116th Street. Old women selling homemade tortillas color the street. At Sam's Famous Pizzeria a long line of hungry people is queuing. Puerto Ricans sell steaming plates of mofongo through a hole in the wall. Jacqueline treats a homeless man to a sandwich. This part of 116th Street is very lively and bursting with authentic street food surprises.

I spend my last evening in New York with Luk, my partner in food crime, in the East Village. We honor this formidable melting pot of cuisines and cultures with a bottle of delicious red wine from Lil' Frankie's pizza place. We appease the remainder of our hunger in Momofuku where we share five appetizers. Once again, David Chang captivates us enormously. Blissfully I browse in my notebook, well aware of the wealth of information I've collected over the past weeks. At this very spot, while I'm still tingling with the energy this fantastic city has given me, I decide which dishes I will put on the menu of my noodle bar in Ghent. For the last time, we take the ferry to Jacqueline's house on Staten Island and watch how Manhattan recedes in the background. This is not goodbye forever; that we know for sure. When New York has you under its spell, you have to return. Back at Jacqueline's place, Luk has a little surprise for me. Grinning broadly, he hands me a flat cardboard box. It contains a neon sign he picked up in Chinatown. In pink and blue fluorescent letters it spells the word: 'OPEN'.

EMPANADA

PASTRY STUFFED WITH MEAT

Ⓛ —Bronx: Jackson Avenue

$ | | | |
0   5   10   15

When we arrived at 3 pm at Piranha's food truck in the Bronx, the whole crew was in a party mood. The free gift of empanada came straight from the heart. Party time!

INGREDIENTS

- 2 tbsp. vegetable oil
- 2 shallots, finely chopped
- 2 cloves garlic
- ¼ tsp. cumin powder
- ¼ tsp. paprika powder
- ¾ lb ground beef
- ½ tsp. salt
- ½ tsp. black pepper
- 4 sheets phyllo dough
  (for 8 empanadas)
- 1 egg, slightly beaten

STEP BY STEP!

\# Preheat the oven to 400 °F.

\# In a pan, combine the oil, shallot and garlic. Cook over low heat, stirring frequently. Add cumin and paprika. Stir. Add the meat, cook over medium heat till the meat is browned. Season with salt and pepper.

\# Cut the pyllo dough in circles of about 4 inches in diameter. Put a heaped tablespoon of beef mix on each circle. Fold the empanada in half, pressing the edges together to seal them. Brush with the slightly beaten egg.

\# Transfer to the oven and bake for 15 minutes till golden brown.

* THERE'S MORE *

In Singapore this dish is called a curry puff, in Vietnam banh goi. Portugese sailors spread this tasty snack all over the world.

aloo tikki chaat
veg. samosa chaat
chicken samosa chaat
biryani
vegetable biryani
chicken biryani
drinks
mango lassi
thums up
soda / water

on same day
/or dairy products;
e vendor

BARNARD

STEP BY STEP!

\# Mix the yogurt with the garlic, ginger and dry herbs. Add 1 tsp. of tomato paste, mix. Add the chicken and lime juice. Mix well, cover, put in the fridge and let marinate for at least 4 hours.

\# Preheat the broiler. Remove the chicken from the marinade and grill for about 15 minutes until almost done. Turn regularly.

\# In a pan, combine the oil, onion and chili powder, cook for a few minutes, stirring occasionally. Add the tomato paste and remaining marinade. Add the chicken cubes and fresh tomato. Stir and cook briefly till the sauce reaches the desired thickness.

\# Garnish with fresh cilantro leaves. Serve with rice and a fresh, chilled salad.

INGREDIENTS

- 1 ¼ cups Greek yogurt
- 4 cloves garlic, finely chopped
- 1 inch fresh ginger, finely chopped
- 1 tsp. cumin powder
- 1 tbsp. garam masala
- 1 tbsp. turmeric powder
- 1 tsp. paprika powder
- 1 tsp. chili powder
- 1 tsp. coriander powder
- 1 tsp. tomato paste
- 4 chicken fillets cut in 1 inch to 1 inch cubes
- juice of 1 lime
- 2 tbsp. vegetable oil
- 1 finely minced onion
- 1 chili pepper, jalapeño
- 1 fresh tomato, chopped
- 1 handful fresh cilantro, chopped

CHICKEN TIKKA

This is one of the most popular dishes in the world, a stellar staple of the Indian cuisine!

★ ★

Ⓛ —Manhattan: Morningside Heights

Ⓢ

GRILLED CHICKEN IN SPICY YOGURT-TOMATO SAUCE

A tandoori is the traditional clay oven in which this chicken is baked.

Recovering after Sandy

On October 29, 2012, the New York area was hit very hard by super storm Sandy. The cleanup and rebuilding were underway while we wrote this book. It will take years to recover. The damage to the city alone was estimated at more then 20 billion dollars. The food sector too suffered great losses. Hundreds of small and larger stores, restaurants, commissaries and refrigerated trucks were destroyed. Thousands in the sector lost their jobs.

Hundreds of thousands of people were without electricity, water and gas. Many had not enough to eat. But just like after 9/11, the city didn't throw in the towel. The needs were so great that the official aid agencies were overwhelmed but thousands of volunteers immediately started helping their neighbors and others. Charity groups, neighborhood organizations and Occupy Sandy, an offshoot of the Occupy Wall Street-movement, stepped in the breach. Members of the NYC Food Truck Association joined the aid action. They sent their trucks, which essentially are mobile kitchens, to the afflicted areas with hot food and water. They were sponsored by private companies but the city too helped pay for the food and gas. In the past year, the city authorities made life more difficult for the food truck owners, imposing more and heavier fines. But in the days after Sandy Mayor Bloomberg thanked the food truck owners for their efficient distribution of more than 275,000 free hot meals. In Hoboken, on the other side of the Hudson in New Jersey, there was a vibrant food truck scene until 2011. Then, under pressure of local restaurant owners, the trucks were prohibited in the city. Sweet revenge! After Sandy the city of Hoboken begged on its Facebook page: 'Have a food truck? Come to Hoboken and help us feed our community.'

Some food truck owners were themselves hit by Sandy. For months it was impossible to stand in downtown, an area that's normally very busy for food trucks, because giant generators, mobile heating equipment, and emergency telephone installations took up all the available parking space.

A little ingenuity can go a long way. In heavily affected neighborhoods like Red Hook, Dumbo, Long Island City and South Street Seaport, most restaurants and bars were not insured for flood damage. Many did not meet the requirements for government subsidies. Instead of giving up, owners launched fund raising actions through internet media like Kickstart and Go Fund My Account. The Lobster Pound in Red Hook estimated it needed 75000 dollar to re-open. Sandy destroyed the entire store and all its content, as well as its commissary across the street. Big Red, the Lobster Pound's food truck, suffered heavy damage too. The store succeeded in collecting enough money by selling, mainly on internet sites, vouchers 'good for one dish in the Lobster Pound or Big Red.' A quarter of the price of the vouchers was earmarked for rebuilding of the store.

Some food truck owners had hoped that their efforts in the weeks after Sandy would be rewarded by a more tolerant attitude on the part of the police and the food inspection. Alas, the honeymoon didn't last very long. In January, food trucks parked at parking meters were again fined and towed. Business as usual.

ADDRESSSES

Pozole
01. MARINA VERA LUZ
Every Sunday in front of the church Shrine of our Lady of Guadalupe
328 West 14th Street, Manhattan
Open 6 am – 3 pm
Mon – Fri on the corner of West 40th Street & 8th Avenue, Manhattan
Open 5 am – 8 am

Papa rellena / morir soñando
02. FORDHAM DOMINICAN CART
Corner of Webster & Fordham Road, Bronx
Open Mon – Sat 10 am – 6 pm

Burrito / pork ribs in green sauce / quesadilla
03. MARIA'S TACO KIOSK
Columbus Square at East Fordham Road, Bronx
Open daily 8 am – 7 pm

Soul food
04. MANNA'S RESTAURANTS
70 West 125th Street
486 Lenox Ave near 134th Street
2331 8th Ave near 125th Street
54 East 125th Street near Madison Avenue
Open Mon – Sat 11 am – 9 pm, Sun 11 am – 8 pm
www.soulfood.com

Soul food
05. THE UNITED HOUSE OF PRAYER FOR ALL PEOPLE CAFETARIA
2320 Frederick Douglass Boulevard & 125th Street, Harlem, Manhattan
Open Mon – Sat 11.30 am – 7 pm, Sun lunch
www.Tuhopfap.com

Oxtail stew / jerk chicken / sorrel
06. VERONICA'S KITCHEN
125 Front Street
Financial District, Manhattan
Open Mon – Fri 10 am – 3 pm

Tajine
07. BISTRO TRUCK
Location changes daily.
Closed end October till early April
www.bistrotruck.com

Greek chicken skewers / feta salad
08. SOUVLAKI TRUCK
Open Mon – Fri 12pm – 9 pm, Sat – Sun 12 pm – 7 pm
Location varies
www.souvlakigr.com

Pizza / scallion pancake

09. SAM'S FAMOUS PIZZERIA
150 East 116th Street (bet Lexington Ave & 3rd Ave) Manhattan
Open daily 7.30 am – 10 pm

Oysters

10. OYSTER BAR RESTAURANT
Lower level Grand Central Terminal, 42nd Street & Vanderbilt Ave, Manhattan
Open Mon – Fri 11.30 am – 10 pm, Sat. 12 pm – 10 pm, closed Sun.
www.oysterbarny.com

Waffle with chili con corne

11. WAFELS & DINGES
www.wafelsanddinges.com

Colombian pancakes / Colombian sweets

12. PALENQUE HOME MADE COLOMBIAN FOOD
*Smorgasburg food market
Kent Avenue, Williamsburg, Brooklyn
Open weekends: April – November 11 am – 6 pm

13. Arepa / cocota
*PALENQUE FOOD TRUCK
Park Ave and 47th or 46th , Manhattan
Open midtown lunch, 12 pm to 4 pm
www.palenquehomemadecolombianfood.com

Spicy lamb noodles / szechuan chicken

14. XIAN FAMOUS FOODS
41- 28 Main Street, Foodcourt
Flushing, Queens
Open daily, 10.30 am – 9.30 pm
www.xianfoods.com

Tempeh sandwich / chocolate brownie

15. THE CINNAMON SNAIL
Park Avenue and 47th or 46th, Manhattan
Open midtown lunch, 12 pm – 4 pm
www.cinnamonsnail.com

Falafel

16. KING OF FALAFEL
Park Avenue and 53rd St, Manhattan
Open Mon – Fri 11 am – 3 pm
www.thekingfalafel.com

Salted beef taco / Mexican sandwich

17. TORTAS NEZA

111th St and Roosevelt Avenue, Queens

Open 6 pm – 10 pm

Osaka pancakes

18. OKDAMAMAN FOOD TRUCK

Park Avenue and 47th or 46th St, Manhattan

Open midtown lunch, 12 am – 4 pm

www.okadamannyc.com

Bulgogi / kimchi

19. WOORIJIP

12 W and 32th St, bet 5th Ave and Broadway, Manhattan

Open daily 8 am – 3 pm

www.woorijipnyc.com

Key lime pie

20. STEVE'S AUTHENTIC KEY LIME PIE

Pier 40, 185 Van Dyke Street

Red Hook, Brooklyn

Open daily, hours vary

www.stevesauthentic.com

Bagel with cream cheese and lox

21. RUSS & DAUGHTERS

179 E Houston Street, between Allen & Orchard Streets

Lower East Side, Manhattan

Open Mon – Fri 8 am – 8 pm, Sat 9 am – 7 pm, Sun 8 am – 5.30 pm

www.russanddaughers.com

Knish

22. YONAH SCHIMMEL KNISH BAKERY

137 E Houston Street, between First & Second Avenues

Lower East Side, Manhattan

Open Mon – Thurs and Sun 9 am – 7 pm, Fri – Sat 9 am – 9 pm

Pastrami sandwich

KATZ'S DELICATESSEN

23. 205 E Houston Street, at Ludlow Street

Lower East Side, Manhattan

Open Mon – Tues 8 am – 9.45pm, Wed – Thurs and Sun 8 am – 11.30 pm,

Fri – Sat 8 am – 2.45 am

www.katzdeli.com

Vealheart satay

24. MOROCHO

1 Union Square West, Manhattan

Open daily 11.30 am – 11 pm

www.facebook.com/morochoNYC

Scallion pancakes
25.   **AA PLAZA**
Under the Flushing- Main Street elevated subway stop (# 7 line)
Flushing, Queens
Open daily 11 am – 8 pm

Tamales / cactus salade
26.   **NIXTAMAL TORTILLERIA**
104- 05, 47th Ave
Corona, Queens
Open Mon – Wed 11 am – 6 pm, Thurs and Sun 11 am – 9 pm, Fri – Sat 11 am – 22 pm

Lobster roll
27.   **RED HOOK LOBSTER POUND**
284 Van Brunt Street, Red Hook, Brooklyn
Open Tues – Thurs and Sun 12 pm – 8 pm, Fri – Sat 12 pm – 10 pm
www.redhooklobster.com

MARKETS EN FOOD COURTS

A.   UNION SQUARE GREENMARKET
North and West sides of Union Square Park
Open Mon, Wed, Fri and Sat, 8 am – 6 pm

B.   EATALY
Shop, food court and restaurants
200 5th Avenue, bet 23th & 24th St, Manhattan
Open daily 10 am – 11 pm
www.eataly.com

C.   ARTHUR AVENUE MARKET
Arthur Avenue & East 187th Street, Bronx
Open Mon – Sat 8 am – 5 pm, closed Sun
www.arthuravenuebronx.com

D.   FOOD COURT
Lower level Grand Central Terminal,
42nd Street & Vanderbilt Ave, Manhattan
Open Mon – Sat 7 am – 9 pm, Sun 11 am – 6 pm

E.   TODD ENGLISH FOOD HALL PLAZA HOTEL
Fifth Avenue (at Central Park South) Manhattan
Open Sun – Thur 11 am – 10 pm, Fri – Sat 11 am – 11 pm
theplazany.com

F.   RED HOOK VENDORS
Red Hook Recreational Area, corner of Bay & Clinton St, Brooklyn
Open Sat – Sun 9 am – 9 pm

G.   CHELSEA MARKET
75 Ninth Avenue, bet 15th & 16th St, Chelsea, Manhattan
Open Mon- Sat 7 am- 9 pm, Sun 8 am- 8 pm
www.chelseamarket.com

H.   SMORGASBURG
2 locations
Sat: East River State Park, Kent Ave & N. 7th Street
Williamsburg Waterfront, Brooklyn
Sun: Tobacco Warehouse, Brooklyn Bridge Park,
Dumbo, Brooklyn
Open April till October, 11 am – 6 pm

I.   NEW WORLD MALL
4021 Main Street
Flushing, Queens
Open daily 9 am – 10 pm
www.newworldmallny.com

REGISTER

TOMATO

TORTILLA

WAFFLES

Colophon

WWW.LANNOO.COM
Register on our website and we will regularly send you a newsletter with
information about new books and interesting, exclusive offers.

TEXT: Tom Vandenberghe, info@eetavontuur.be
and Jacqueline Goossens, www.jacquelinegoossens.com
PHOTOGRAPHY: Luk Thys, luk@foodphoto.be
DESIGN: Natasja Billiau, info@prezent.nu
TRANSLATION: Tom Ronse

CHECK OUT: www.ilikestreetfood.com

If you have observations or questions, please contact our editorial office:
redactielifestyle@lannoo.com

Third printrun

© Lannoo Publishers, Tielt, Belgium, 2013
D/2013/45/321 – NUR 442
ISBN: 978 94 014 0369 6

NUC..
JUGO..
"Pepina

Try our
"New Juice
CUCumber

de
Mango